KATIE & ALEX

KATIE & ALEX
THE INSIDE STORY

Alison Maloney

MICHAEL O'MARA BOOKS LIMITED

First published in Great Britain in 2010 by
Michael O'Mara Books Limited
9 Lion Yard
Tremadoc Road
London SW4 7NQ

A CIP cat

This book has   atie
P

Papers used   l,
recyclable prod   ests.
The manufacturing processes conform to the environmental
regulations of the country of origin.

ISBN: 978-1-84317-487-5

1 3 5 7 9 10 8 6 4 2

Designed and typeset by E-Type

Printed and bound in Great Britain by Cox & Wyman,
Reading, Berks

www.mombooks.com

CONTENTS

CONTENTS

INTRODUCTION

'S HE DOESN'T WANT to live off-camera, much less talk. There's nothing to say off-camera. Why would you say something if it's off-camera? What point is there existing?'

Warren Beatty famously scolded Madonna with these words in her documentary *Truth or Dare*. Yet, even by Madonna's standards, no relationship has been as public as that of Katie Price and Alex Reid.

From the moment they met to the moment they married, the highs and lows of their relationship have been relentlessly caught on camera. Katie chose a TV show to dump her new man in November 2009; and it was another reality show, *Celebrity Big Brother*, which catapulted the cage fighter to fame on his own terms and on which he publicly declared, 'I love Katie Price!' It was also the programme that turned public opinion in his favour and led to the whirlwind Vegas wedding, which took place less than a week after he had left the *CBB* house.

But, despite the relative speed of their union, the high-profile pair have not had an easy route to the altar. After all, they met when Katie was going through a painful divorce from Australian singer Peter Andre, the father of two of her three children. The bitter recriminations and public bickering between the former lovers sent Katie close to the edge on occasion and, while Pete claimed victory over his ex-wife at the PR game, Katie became skilled at putting on a brave face. But as her new romance flourished, caring Alex was often the one who was there to pick up the pieces of her broken heart.

If the millionaire model took her fair share of the flack, it was also tough for media novice Alex. Not only did he watch his new love go through hell, but the press were soon uncovering his secret fetish and printing lurid details of his life, as told by ex-girlfriends. Attacked on martial arts sites – the community he had fought all his life to be respected by – jeered at on a daily basis by the tabloids and eventually dumped on national TV, Alex had been thrust into the limelight in the worst way. Less than two months after his lowest point, though, he was crowned the *Celebrity Big Brother* winner, and heading for marriage.

'We've been together for seven months,' he said to *OK!* magazine, just before their wedding in February, 'and been through more than most couples go through in a lifetime.'

From the moment they met and fell in love, it was a rollercoaster ride, from which both would emerge shaken, but stronger and more determined than ever to be together – for life.

In *Katie & Alex: The Inside Story*, we follow the ups and downs of the most extraordinary romance in showbiz – from the first date to the Las Vegas chapel where they finally became man and wife.

CHAPTER ONE

THE LOVE STORY BEGINS

As she got ready for best pal Michelle Heaton's thirtieth birthday party in July 2009, Katie Price had one thing on her mind. She had recently split from husband Peter Andre, had just declared to Piers Morgan on a prime-time TV show that she was 'back on the market' – and she was out to show her ex exactly what he was missing.

As a result, she had selected a knockout black dress – consisting of a tiny tutu and a figure-sculpting corset – that emphasized her two most famous assets to eye-popping proportions. She made her face up, put on some killer heels and smiled at herself in the mirror. She was ready to party.

With the eyes of the world's press upon her, she arrived at the Studio Valbonne club in London and declared, 'I'm going to have some fun.' Little did she know that this was the night she would meet the next Mr Right.

For at the beginning of the evening, Katie was introduced by her personal trainer Sol Gilbert to cage fighter and bit-part actor Alex Reid. Her new acquaintance's muscle-bound looks hardly came as a surprise to her, however.

Weeks before, she had spotted a picture of Alex at Sol's Brighton gym, Fight Skool, where she had been training since April. She asked Sol about him, asked for his number and began sending Alex texts.

The helpful trainer, who happened to be Alex's best friend, decided to play Cupid, and invited his pal along to Michelle's birthday bash, where Katie, as one of the birthday girl's closest chums, was guaranteed to be in attendance.

'Alex was at a loose end, so I invited him. The chemistry was instant,' Sol told *The People* two weeks later. And he revealed that it wasn't just a sexual buzz, saying that Katie immediately felt at ease in Alex's presence. Against type, the cage fighter is actually a chilled and naturally laid-back guy and, perhaps because of his acting past, he is not the type to be at all star-struck by celebrities, which was a breath of fresh air to someone as iconic as Katie had become.

Of course, his height – Alex is over 6 feet tall – and bulging muscles were not exactly a turn-off, either.

After a night of flirting at the London venue, Alex went back to Katie's seven-bedroom mansion in Surrey – for security reasons, of course.

'They did their own thing that night,' explained Sol to *The People*. 'They were bowled over by each other. Katie's security man Danny wasn't [at the club], so Alex stepped in. He went in her car back with her and stayed the night. The next day, Katie said she had a great night, that he is a great guy, and asked me how I knew they would have a lot in common.

'I simply told her that I know them both and if there was anyone she was going to hit it off with, it would be him.'

Alex told his pal that, although they'd had a wonderful time, they hadn't slept together that night. Sol told *The People* that Katie had refused, wanting to make sure Alex was the right person first. However, he believed that they did 'seal the deal' a week later.

But in a recent *OK!* interview, Katie confessed that she hadn't waited at all. 'I got it off him the first night,' she revealed to the magazine. 'I'd been looking at pictures of him and texting him before that, though. Then I met Alex, slept with him the first night, and have stayed with him since. How could I resist the power of Alex?'

It seemed that Alex was having trouble resisting the power of Katie. The days that followed their first date were later televised in her reality show *What Katie Did Next*. The programme showed a clearly besotted Alex trailing his famous lover around the country as she promoted her new novel, *Sapphire*. As Katie attempted to get ready for a photo shoot, the new man in her life couldn't keep his hands off her, kissing and cuddling her even as she was having her face made up.

Two days after their first meeting, Katie threw an early birthday dinner for Alex – who would turn thirty-four in August – and some friends at her home. 'I've decided what I'm going to cook,' she told the cameras excitedly. 'Chicken Chasseur: because I can put it in the pot with some herbs and leave it. Then I'll do mashed potato.'

As Katie played the hostess with the mostest, dressed in tiny red shorts, football socks and a skintight T-shirt, Alex looked on proudly. And the sequinned message across her chest, reading 'Secret Lover', gave him reason to smile as well. 'You like that, don't you?' she teased.

It was a private joke, meant to allude to the fact that the press, who usually hounded her every move, had not yet been told about the relationship, which the duo would continue to deny for a few more days. Indeed, on a TV show the next day, Katie refuted the idea that she was in any relationship, despite reports that she had bought Alex a £4,000 Cartier watch as a birthday gift.

On 25 July, a week after they met, visitors at the Malmaison Hotel in Liverpool reported seeing the couple canoodling and going up to Katie's room together. But a pal said, 'He has been brought in for security, nothing more.'

Katie's own spokesman commented, 'He makes Katie feel secure; he is a trained cage fighter and acts as extra security for her.

'She said she wants him there to keep her safe and he did accompany her into her room in Liverpool.'

But behind the scenes, feelings were already running high. On their way to film a part in the new Freeview ad, sitting next to Alex in the back of the car, Katie mused on the fact that she was moving on from her painful split with Peter Andre, the father of her two youngest children.

'It's going to be an interesting week because at the weekend the papers were stirred up a bit about what Pricey's been up to,' she said on *What Katie Did Next*. 'I'm going through a divorce. Everyone knows that he [Pete] can do what he likes and I can do what I like. What am I supposed to do, sit around? You don't know who you're going to fall for, when or how.'

Alex agreed, saying, 'We're both adults and as you get older, you get a bit cynical about that four-letter word, L-O-V-E, but it still happens – and very quickly.' Realizing he had just confessed his deepest feelings after only a week, Alex laughed self-consciously, quipping, 'Did I just say something?' But the fact was, the spark between the two was electric.

At the shoot, Katie's best pal and make-up artist Gary Cockerill chatted with her about the full-on nature of the new relationship, wondering if, with all these sparks flying about, it was all going to be too much for the newly single glamour girl. Though Katie was openly celebrating Alex's sexual prowess, calling him a 'real man', Gary was concerned about whether the chemistry that worked so well between the sheets would be as successful in everyday life.

'While that combination [of the two of you together] might be amazing in the bedroom,' he persisted on *What Katie Did Next*, 'is it going to be too much, too intense?'

But Katie waved away his concerns, convinced that she and Alex had something special. 'I always believe if something feels right, go for it,' she explained, before admitting that their burgeoning relationship could 'definitely' become a fully-fledged love affair with all the feelings to match. As it had been for Alex, the fact that the pair had only known each other a week was a small detail in the face of their overwhelming emotions.

Katie also revealed to Gary that she wasn't just bowled over by Alex's looks and abilities in the bedroom: he understood her. She said, 'He knows how to put me in my place, already. He doesn't stand for any shit. I like that. I need that.'

For someone like Katie, to whom, all too often, people simply said 'yes', however madcap her schemes and ideas, it was a refreshing change to have someone who didn't roll over the minute she made a demand.

Mutual friend and matchmaker Sol Gilbert joined in the love fest by telling *The People* that the couple's future was mapped out as soon as their eyes had met.

'The moment they met, it was obvious they were made for one another,' he said. 'There is absolutely no doubt they are besotted boyfriend and girlfriend and looking forward to a future together. I think she believes he could be The One, even though it's early days.'

As a close friend of both parties, Sol had a unique insight into their relationship, and wasn't swayed by the gossip and speculation that had swamped the couple even from their first meeting. 'People might think it's a rebound thing, but I know it's not,' he said. 'I have known Alex for nearly seven years and I have never seen him fall for a woman like he has for Katie.'

Unlike Alex, Katie was used to her relationships being the subject of showbiz gossip columns – and the majority of her ex-lovers had been in the public eye themselves. So far she had clocked up two footballers, three singers and a Gladiator in her lovers' list. Unknown Alex was not her usual high-profile target.

Katie's most serious previous relationship, before her marriage to Peter Andre, was with Another Level boy-band member Dane Bowers, who later shared the *Celebrity Big Brother* house with Alex in January 2010.

The couple met in 1998 and split in 2000, while Katie was pregnant with their child. The devastated model had an abortion and, even after the divorce from Peter, she claimed that the break-up with Dane was the most painful for her. At her lowest point, she even took an overdose to escape from her torment.

'I've always said that when I split up from Dane, that was the worst break-up I've ever had in my life,' she told *OK!* magazine. 'I did the overdose and, from that day, I always said I'd never, ever, ever let a man do that to me again. I know people find it hard to believe, but when you've been hurt that bad and it takes two years to get over someone, I can't let emotion get to me.'

Coincidentally, nine years later, Dane announced his split from his wife Chrissy just two days before Katie and Peter went their separate ways. Shortly afterwards, he and Katie met up for the first time since their break-up and worked through a lot of their old animosity.

'I can't explain how weird it felt to see Kate again and to realize I still care deeply for her,' Dane revealed to *The People* at the time. 'I discovered a part of me still loves her and probably always will.'

It was a reconciliation that had been a long time coming, but one that laid to rest plenty of old ghosts.

Before Dane, and any surgical enhancement to her figure, Katie was briefly engaged to Warren Furman, a star of the TV show *Gladiators*, who went under the name of Ace. The couple parted ways after a series of jealous rows.

After Dane, a brief fling with Manchester United player Teddy Sheringham in 2000 was followed by a longer relationship with his teammate Dwight Yorke, the father of Katie's first child, Harvey, who was born in May 2002.

Harvey was born blind, with a rare condition called septo-optic dysplasia, which affects the development of his optic nerve. He was later found to be autistic, and also suffering from a condition that makes walking difficult. Katie has never shied away from his disabilities and in fact has won widespread commendation for the way in which she has coped with the diagnosis and Harvey's special needs.

The romance with Harvey's father ended while Katie was pregnant; soon after, a one-night stand with seventeen-year-old *Pop Idol* star Gareth Gates hit the headlines. Things went from bad to worse when Dwight claimed he was unsure if he was Harvey's dad and demanded a paternity test. The DNA exam proved he was indeed Harvey's biological father. Nevertheless, after a failed attempt to patch things up on a Caribbean holiday, Dwight and Katie permanently went their separate ways.

Katie then went on to date Matt Peacock, a tanning salon worker, who later married her arch rival, fellow glamour model Jodie Marsh, in a stunt for a reality TV show.

Shortly before she entered the jungle for her first stint on *I'm a Celebrity … Get Me Out of Here!* in 2004 – during which she famously met future husband Peter Andre – Katie was happily dating unknown Scott Sullivan. But the frustrated lad could only watch as she openly flirted with the Australian beefcake on national TV, later telling *Closer* magazine, 'She's hurt me so much. I've been humiliated in front of the world. I'm totally confused.'

In an uncanny foretaste of the treatment Katie

would later mete out to Alex after her second bout on *I'm a Celebrity*, she dumped Scott the minute she left the jungle.

In Peter, with whom Katie fell in love during the 2004 series, it looked like she had at last found the man of her dreams. Their romance moved her media exposure up several notches. In fact, that would be an understatement. This was a whole new level of celebrity.

A lucrative deal with *OK!* magazine saw the couple's fairy-tale wedding, complete with Cinderella coach and pink Barbie wedding dress, splashed over several pages and two editions. The newlyweds also landed themselves a series of ITV2 reality shows, beginning with *When Jordan Met Peter* and ending, as their marriage was falling apart in 2009, with *Katie and Peter: Stateside*. They also graced the covers of many glossy magazines, and of course the tabloids, and published their autobiographies – several volumes, in Katie's case. Having made the transition from glamour girl to business-woman, and with her beautifully manicured fingers in countless different pies, Katie found herself becoming a major icon.

From the start, Pete bonded with Katie's disabled

son Harvey and proved to be a fantastic father figure. In June 2005, their first child together, Junior Savva Andreas Andre, was born, and a daughter, Princess Tiaamii Crystal Esther Andre, followed in June 2007.

But behind the scenes, the happy family was not quite so happy. The couple announced their split on 11 May 2009, and Katie was devastated, not least because she had miscarried their third child just weeks before and was in a very emotional state. It later emerged that the marriage had been in trouble for a while. Katie and Peter had tried counselling, but to no avail. Separation, and consequently divorce, became inevitable.

A month after the break-up was formally announced, Katie was to make the first 'wrong' move in the media battle between the former lovers that was set to become a bitter slanging match. As a clearly sad Pete took the three children to Cyprus to enjoy a family break with his parents, Savva and Thea, Katie took an entourage of pals to the clubbers' Mecca of Ibiza for a booze-fuelled week away. As Pete was pictured in the papers kissing Harvey, and playing with the kids on the beach, a scantily clad Kate was snapped with a series of muscle-bound clubbers, and looking bleary-eyed, coming out of nightclubs in the early hours of the morning.

Eight months later, she defended her holiday on a Radio 1 show, saying she never went 'off the rails'.

'Are you telling me that no other woman would go on holiday [after a break-up]?' she asked DJ Chris Moyles. 'Why not? I had so much fun. I don't regret that holiday. It's the best holiday I'd had for a long time.'

'But you knew the papers would follow you,' she was reminded.

However, having been a media target all her adult life, Katie was not about to start letting the press dictate her actions. 'I can't live my life round what the papers are going to say,' she said bluntly. 'How sad would that be? If I'm worried all the time. I'm not going to let that rule my life.'

But although Katie was all too familiar with being pilloried in the papers, her split from Peter was opening up a whole new can of worms. As she partied wildly, and he stayed at home playing the doting dad, the media came down firmly on the side of Team Andre. And there they would stay for many months yet.

While Katie's romances had filled column inches for years, Alex's previous relationships had all been long-term, private affairs. All that was about to change.

CHAPTER TWO

A WHOLE NEW WORLD

WHILE THE ROMANCE between Kate and Alex had stirred up some intense feelings in a relatively short time, Katie kept it low-key when she finally broke her silence to the media, one week after they met.

'I'm having lots of fun at the moment, which I think I deserve after everything I have been through lately,' she told *The People*.

And she added, '[Alex] is a fighter. He's a bit like me in that respect.'

The throwaway comment hit the nail on the head when it came to the similarities in the couple's background. Both had to fight for the futures they desired – and both showed a steely determination to succeed.

As Jordan, Katie clawed her way up from a chance appearance as a Page Three girl – filling in at the last minute for someone who dropped out of a shoot – to become the most famous glamour model in Britain, as well as a TV star with her own series, a bestselling author and a millionaire business-woman, with her own range of lingerie, perfume, equestrian clothing and even bed linen.

Alex, one of six kids brought up in Aldershot, Hampshire by builder Bob Reid and wife Carol, has been determined to be a cage fighter since he was a young lad, and he has pursued that ambition regard-less of the unorthodox career choice or the toughness of his chosen discipline. Over the years, he has built up a huge amount of respect in the mixed martial arts community, where he is known as The Reidinator.

In a recent interview, mum Carol confessed that she never liked him fighting – and that she thought he was too soft-hearted for the career.

'I tried to talk him out of it. But that's what he wanted to be when he was just fourteen. It's a shame,' she told Adam Lee-Potter of the *Sunday Mirror*. 'He used to be such a good-looking man. His nose and ears are dreadful now.

'And he's too gentle to be a fighter, really. That's one of his problems in the ring. He still gets upset when he knocks someone down.'

Like Katie, Alex has sought fame in other fields,

too, working as a stunt double in Hollywood movie *Saving Private Ryan* and taking on various acting roles. His most successful stint was as amoral footballer Jason Cunliffe in the Channel 4 soap *Hollyoaks* from 2001 to 2002.

When the two met, in the summer of 2009, they were both recovering following the breakdown of serious long-term relationships. Katie was going through a divorce from Australian singer Peter Andre, her husband of three and a half years and the father of her two youngest children, Junior and Princess Tiaamii. The former couple, who met on jungle show *I'm a Celebrity … Get Me Out of Here!* in 2004, had split in May and been involved in a very public war of words ever since.

Alex, meanwhile, had recently split from teacher Marie Thornett, whom he had been dating, off and on, for ten years. And as he and Katie basked in the warm glow of new love, it seemed their exes were not quite so happy.

When asked about pics of Katie with her new man, Peter told *The Sun*, 'Nothing fazes me anymore. All I'll say is that the way she behaves is different from the way I'd behave.'

Marie, however, was not so diplomatic, claiming

that Alex was due to be on holiday with her when he first got together with Katie.

'Alex was supposed to be with me in Spain, instead he was groping her in a nightclub,' she was quoted as saying in the *News of the World*. 'We planned to spend the rest of our lives together and now it's in ruins – thanks to Jordan.

'What those two have done to me is cruel beyond words. They've thought of nobody but themselves. I've cried almost non-stop since I found out. I can never forgive them.'

Alex's friends later denied that the pair were still together when he met Katie, saying that he had split with Marie early in 2009.

These rumblings in the media didn't appear to trouble the happy new couple, though. In the last two weeks of July, Katie and Alex were inseparable, as he travelled with her to Liverpool, Manchester and London on her book-signing tour.

Nine days after they met, Alex made a modern-day public announcement: changing his Facebook status from 'single' to 'in a relationship'. Realizing he had to get back to his own life, he also wrote, 'Time for me to get back in the gym! Gotta get this girl out of my head for at least an hour!'

From the start, Alex was keen to shoot down accusations that he was fame-hungry and hooking up with Katie solely to launch a career in the spotlight. 'I am serious about Kate, I have never felt like this about someone before,' he confessed to the *Daily Star*.

Certainly his friend Sol Gilbert had high hopes for the union, even before a fortnight was out. Sol revealed that the idea of bonding with Katie's kids would not faze the thirty-four-year-old cage fighter, as Alex was desperate to settle down and have children of his own. And Sol reckoned he had finally found the right girl to start a family with.

'Alex is one of those people who has wanted to meet the right person and settle down for years,' he said to *The People*. 'He is a family man; he is great with my two sons. That is definitely the thing missing from his life, and Katie is the person he wants to share that with.'

And Sol was convinced that their family would be a remarkably successful and joyous one, predicting that protective Alex would be a fantastic father and the perfect foil to Katie, whom he described as a 'very maternal and motherly woman'.

Within a week, Alex got the chance to put those

fatherly skills to the test when he was introduced to Katie's three beloved children. Happily, the quartet seemed to get on like a house on fire. Katie cooked roast lamb for lunch and invited her new man, together with their mutual friend Sol and his wife, to share the meal in her Surrey home. Alex joked with the kids and played games with them, to the delight of their mum. She was particularly happy that seven-year-old Harvey, her severely disabled son by footballer Dwight Yorke, took to Alex.

'Harvey bounced on him yesterday and laughed, and for Harvey to do that, he must like him,' she told her friend Gary Cockerill on her TV show.

And Katie was quick to highlight the seriousness of her new liaison. Unlike the Ibiza dalliances, her affair with Alex had all the hallmarks of being a more permanent partnership. As Katie said to Gary, 'It's not like I'm just shagging him, I'm in a relationship with the guy.'

Dad Peter was not so happy with the situation, and claimed his four-year-old son had started asking questions about his mum sharing a bed with another man. 'It was a knife in the heart. Not just that, it was a knife, a twist and a lift,' he told *The Sun* in early August. 'I heard [in the media that]

Junior had been asking why Mummy was in bed with another man. I didn't believe it. I just thought it was kids saying things.

'But Junior has said it to me since. It's something a four-year-old should not be saying.

'I don't want to look like I am using the kids to have a dig at her, but they should never, ever be exposed to that kind of thing. For a child to see that is one thing. But for a child to see it in the bed that he only knows Mummy and Daddy to sleep in? That is disgusting. That to me is the lowest blow ever. And for Junior to come and speak to me about it ... He is only four!'

But Pete vowed to put his two children, and their older brother Harvey, first at all times. 'The three most important people in my life are Harvey, Junior and Princess, and as long as they are looked after, I can't control what anyone else does.'

Shocked Katie immediately denied that Junior had seen anything inappropriate.

After Katie's whirlwind book tour, the blissfully happy couple decided to take some time out with a holiday in Marbella, where they hired a luxury villa. The press had an absolute field day as the passionate duo threw caution to the wind and shocked holidaymakers at an exclusive golf resort with their poolside antics. Still in the first flush of romance, they couldn't keep their hands off each other and Alex openly groped his topless girlfriend in the pool.

In one famous photo, as Katie chilled out with a massage, Alex crept up on her, signalled for the masseuse to take a hand away, and replaced it with his own. Cheekily, that hand then roamed onto his girlfriend's bottom and gave it a pinch. Initially shocked at what she thought was a very forward masseuse, Katie laughed uproariously when she discovered that the wandering hand belonged to her lover.

Stories in the papers back home, however, had turned the tide and the tabloids were now reporting whispers from 'friends' that Katie was about to give her muscle-bound man the elbow. It was time to put the record straight.

'People are saying it's too soon for me to have a new boyfriend,' she wrote in her *OK!* column. 'But it's nearly four months since me and Pete split up – and remember he walked out on me. I am a human being and am entitled to my own life since he walked out.'

And, as anyone can see, Katie Price is not someone who lets opportunities pass her by. The model's whole approach to life can be summed up as *'carpe diem'* – 'seize the day'. In her eyes, Alex was the best opportunity to come her way in a long time and she was grabbing him – literally – with both hands. 'I'm not going to wait three months or six months. If something's right, go for it,' she enthused on *What Katie Did Next*.

In the light of the negative press reports, Alex's mum Carol was swift to jump to her son's defence too. 'He's in love with Katie,' she confirmed to the *Daily Star*. 'They're young and they're happy. They're not hurting anyone.'

The following weekend, the couple put on a united front at a vow-renewal ceremony for Katie's friend Gary and his partner Phil Turner, which was filmed for Living TV's *Four Weddings* show. The three children also came along to the lavish bash at posh Syon Park in west London.

Typically, 'best woman' Katie caused a stir when she walked down the aisle in a white wedding dress and tiara. But the fashion item that garnered the most attention was a new ring – worn on her wedding finger. The press seized on the symbolic jewellery and there was widespread speculation about wedding plans and even babies.

But Katie's camp was swift to quash the rumours. 'There are no plans for marriage,' said a spokesman. 'I am sure Kate was just wearing that ring on that finger because that's the one it fit.

'She had a lovely time at the renewal of vows and she and Alex are fine – there is no truth in the break-up rumours. But the baby plans are categorically, one hundred per cent untrue.'

Katie changed into a less demure skintight evening dress for Gary and Phil's reception at the Mayfair Hotel, where she interrupted the professional singers to belt out a number for the guests, at Gary's request.

Clearly privy to his girlfriend's rehearsals, Alex joked to the camera: 'I've heard it a million times already. I'm looking forward to it being over!'

While enjoying the day with Alex, Katie hinted on *What Katie Did Next* that she could see a similar event in her own future, saying, 'I know I'll get married again.' And the significance of marriage wasn't far from her mind. Despite the break-up with Pete, she still aspired to a lifelong partnership: 'I felt like I was failure [getting divorced] because when you marry someone, you do it for life, and [my marriage to Pete] wasn't for life. I felt I did the best I could, but it didn't work.'

Meanwhile, the war of words with her soon-to-be-ex-husband Peter continued. In mid August, Katie bared her soul to the *News of the World* about their marriage, saying, 'I tried for five years to be something I suppose I wasn't really, just because I wanted the marriage to work. I was in love with Pete. But you end up rebelling.'

She admitted that the couple had been faking their united front for almost two years. 'For the past two years, things weren't good. We had marriage counselling.

'And I really tried. I was never going to leave him because I believe you try and make things work. But now I'm not in that situation, it's as if a big weight has been lifted off. I think, "Would I ever go back?" There's just no way I could.'

With her private life in turmoil – a rollercoaster ride of emotions ranging from euphoria over her relationship with Alex to despair over her increasingly bitter fight with Peter – friends began to get concerned that she would spiral into a Britney Spears-style meltdown. But Katie kept her eye on

43

the ball and, in the midst of the fallout, she proved to be as shrewd a businesswoman as ever.

On 12 August, as interest in her love life peaked, it was announced that Katie was starting her own production company. Pricey Media, formed with former ITV talent supremo Mark Wagman, announced that its first project would be the follow-up to reality show *Katie and Peter*, this time turning the spotlight on Katie's post-split life. The six-part series, made in conjunction with ITV, was to be called *What Katie Did Next* and would screen in the autumn season of 2009. Filming had been going on throughout the summer and Alex was inevitably to become a major star of the show.

CHAPTER THREE

THE PRICE OF FAME

THE RECENT OBSESSION with celebrity has seen a generation of youngsters hungry for fame at any cost, and Katie is the queen of the celebrity scene. With her every move documented on TV and in the newspapers, dating Katie comes with 'a whole new world' attached.

Within days of Alex and Katie's liaison becoming public, Alex's ex Danielle Sims had sold her story to the *News of the World*, spilling the beans on their 'great sex life'.

She did point out his softer side, however, saying, 'When I was upset, he could be very tender. He would stroke my hair, give me a massage, or we'd just snuggle up on the sofa and watch a film.'

The ex, who had a three-year relationship with Alex that ended in 2007, ultimately gave the couple her blessing. 'I think he and Jordan are well suited because they are a feisty, sexy pair,' she said.

Alex's other ex was not in the mood to be so pleasant. Marie Thornett damned Alex as 'desperate to be famous', saying to the *Daily Star*, 'He's been working towards that for the last ten years. Being with Jordan is a great opportunity for him to get known.' But the fighter seemed genuinely in love and took his new-found notoriety in his sizeable stride.

At the beginning of August, Alex joined Katie and the children for a day out in Stanmer Park, near Brighton, where Katie used to ride as a child. The party set out for their 'getaway day' in Katie's new toy – a £120,000 30-foot custom-built horsebox in hot pink, with her trademark tiara motif decorating the sides.

Although she was driving the most conspicuous vehicle on the road, Katie – who had been hoping for a stress-free family day out – was annoyed to find the paparazzi trailing behind.

'There are a load of paps following us. There never is a quiet place in my world,' she told Alex, in a conversation that was later broadcast on *What Katie Did Next*. 'You'll get sick of this. You'll leave me because of all this.'

Alex, however, didn't mind in the slightest – even when they arrived at their destination and found their every move being trailed, as the photographers set up camp for the day in a spot with a prize view of the family's antics. In fact, not only did Alex seem unconcerned by their presence, but – after playing with the children on the grass for a time – he came up with a novel approach to dealing with the photographers on the hill.

'Let's get the paps,' he suggested, picking up a tennis racquet. 'All the Priceys against all the paps.'

Then he challenged the four press men to a game of softball with the family – as long as they put down their cameras for a while. The ploy was a resounding success, a good day out was had by all, including the kids, and the photographers went home tired, happy and, most importantly, on side.

To Katie, who had been in the public eye from the age of seventeen, it was merely another day in the media circus. For Alex, it was a test, an indication of how well he would cope with life in the spotlight. He passed with flying colours and seemed to enjoy every second of the attention.

Little did he know, the ride was about to get a whole lot rougher. Five weeks into the relationship … and the speculation about the romance turned to speculation about Alex himself. Inevitably, the tabloids were ready to dish some dirt.

First, spurned lover Marie gave an interview to the *Sunday Mirror*, in which she accused him of being a vain exhibitionist. 'Alex has only one real love – and that's himself,' she said. 'Fame and fortune are what drives him. He's vain and vacuous. I believe they are made for each other.'

She revealed that he loved to strip off, even in front of her family, and waxed every inch of his body. 'He's worse than any woman when it comes to beauty,' she continued. 'He loves sunbeds. He's always in the garden topping up his tan. And his nails are immaculate. He has mirrored wardrobes in his bedroom, there's a mirror on the wall and on the window-sill.' But she also said he was 'romantic and deeply sensitive' as well as being a 'thoughtful lover'.

'Jordan should be very cautious,' she concluded. 'He might think he's in love – but he is also in love with the idea of being rich and famous.'

The same weekend, Katie went to watch Alex compering a fight night in Hove, where he publicly declared, 'I love you, lady,' to his new woman.

But the evening ended badly: a 4 a.m. visit to a kebab shop saw the couple confronted by a member of the public, who screamed, 'You are a slag!' at Katie. The woman was dragged away by security men from a nearby nightclub, but the whole episode had a nasty feel to it. Reality was starting to intrude on the love bubble in which Katie and Alex had been living for the past couple of weeks – and an even more explosive incident was about to rock the duo's new-found happiness, as ugly rumours hit the news-stands, fuelled by Alex's latest career move.

That week, the sometime actor's new role in gangster movie *Killer Babe* (formerly known as *Killer Bitch*), which also stars former gangster Dave Courtney and ex-football hooligan Cass Pennant, came under close scrutiny. Things turned sour when he was accused of being involved in hard-core porn. Footage showing him having violent sex with actress Yvette Rowland, before apparently throttling her, led to national outrage.

Alex's spokesman issued a statement: 'He has been shooting a gangster film that has a pornographic scene in it. But it is not a porn film.'

Katie, meanwhile, was forced to defend her boyfriend on *GMTV*, saying, 'One newspaper claimed he was doing a rape scene in a porn film, which is absolute rubbish … It's a gangster movie.'

The couple were really upset by the stories, which broke as Katie was about to leave the country to promote her equestrian clothing range abroad. 'I'm seriously stressed,' she said on *What Katie Did Next*. 'We're getting seriously bad press.'

Alex was philosophical about the tabloid reports, but was emotional as he insisted that anything the papers revealed would have little impact on their burgeoning romance. 'The thing with me and Katie and all this bad press is that Katie knows everything there is to know about me,' he said. 'It's still not nice when you see it – your dirty laundry in public – but what's going on between us … only we know that.'

Then, close to tears, he added, 'I'm getting all soppy – we look at each other, in each other's eyes at night, and that's real, that's magic.'

The intensity of feeling was clear to see. Admittedly, Alex and Katie were undoubtedly caught up in the heady early days of a new romance, but the pressure they were under could have made a weaker couple crumble and split. Instead, the pressure seemed to make them stronger than ever. Little did they know it, but that would become a theme of their relationship over the coming months.

For her part, Katie wanted to show that strength

and togetherness to the world – more so than ever at this difficult time. As a result of the bad publicity, three hours before flying to Spain for her equestrian clothing promotional trip, Katie decided that Alex was coming with her.

Life in the spotlight had taught her that her every move would be scrutinized and analysed, and she knew she needed to be seen to be standing by her man. She was all too aware that any separation now would simply lead to more mean rumours. 'I don't want them to say, if I go on my own, "Oh look, she's not with Alex, she's pissed off and they're not together." I can only stick by him and help the situation,' she explained on *What Katie Did Next*.

In Spain, Katie helped to attract the biggest crowd the organizers had ever seen at a polo match, despite previous guests including the Duchess of York. With Alex keeping a watchful eye, Katie signed hundreds of autographs, but eventually she couldn't take any more and called an end to the signing session.

Frustrated by questions about Alex's film from the media, Katie then vented with a much-needed behind-the-scenes rant. She reckoned she'd identified a motive for the constant public mud-raking:

to discredit Alex to such an extent that Katie might dump him, leaving the way clear for a host of patronizing 'I told you so' columns about how the relationship was never going to work, and how Katie had been irresponsible to introduce her new boyfriend to her young children.

But with the strength of Katie's feelings for Alex – and her hardened approach when it came to press stories – the effect of the media stirring was a bit of a damp squib, though it did fire Katie up on the subject of being a mother with a life. Like many women, she didn't see why the two had to be mutually exclusive. A lot of the criticism levelled at Alex – and Katie – was filtered through the prism of Katie's single motherhood, and the model was frustrated that moving on and having a personal life seemed to invite negative comment just because she had children. 'So I'm a mummy in the day, and as soon as they're in bed, I'm not an angel. So what? I'm having fun,' she said on *What Katie Did Next*.

Alex, with Katie on his lap, was keen to back her up. 'Why do you have to fit into any box?' he asked. 'You do what you want to do and that's why I love you.'

But despite the feisty, independent stance, behind

the scenes, Katie was beginning to worry that she was losing her popularity in the wake of her split from Pete. She was concerned that 'Team Andre' was scoring too many points against 'Team Price'. On several occasions, including the disturbing incident in the kebab shop, Katie had been greeted with abuse or boos from the public and, while she put on a defiant front and laughed it off with such quips as 'I'm like Marmite – you either love me or hate me,' she was beginning to get seriously frustrated and upset by the public reaction.

Occasionally she vented her anger on her Twitter page, railing, 'I'm just seeing someone I like spending time with! Whilst pete has children I dont always want to be sat at home on my own ... I'm only human! I'm away with my friends relaxing while pete was due to have chilren this week ... it seems whatever i do is wrong!' And on seeing pictures of her ex taking the children fruit-picking, she tweeted, 'Strawberry picking... what next?'

Pete upped the ante by giving a series of interviews about the break-up, in which he confessed that he would have been willing to take her back had it not been for the way she had behaved since the split.

'I've finally accepted our marriage is over. I've

shed my last tear,' he said to the *Mirror*. 'It's been nearly four months, but I'm now in the light at the end of the tunnel.

'Nothing about her can shock me any more. For the first time, it doesn't make me mad or upset. It simply washes over me. Once it would have hurt me so, so much, but not now.'

In a reference to Alex, he conceded, 'I'm not bothered who Kate dates or who she's in a relationship with, as long as it doesn't affect my children.'

But he pulled a masterstroke when he himself vowed to stay single, for the sake of the children, until the divorce was finalized. 'I have kept to this celibacy vow and will do so until the day our divorce is made official,' he revealed. 'I know I can look back at this in years to come and feel I did the right thing and acted in the right way. You've got to think long term and think of the kids, which is what I've tried to do.

'I don't want them growing up and reading about things I got up to after splitting from their mum. Unfortunately, I cannot control what other people do.'

A 90-minute documentary, *Peter Andre: Going It Alone*, was screened on ITV in mid August and began with the revelation that he was too traumatized in the first month after the split to let the cameras in. Emotions ran high throughout the show and one scene saw the Aussie singer break down in tears in Ikea as he shopped for furniture for his new home in Brighton with brother Michael and manager Claire. Katie, an expert at manipulating the media all her life, had been outplayed and much of the public sympathy was coming down firmly on the side of Team Andre.

It was time for Katie to fight back and, shrewd as ever, she identified a surprising secret weapon – Alex himself. She already knew that the 'vicious cage fighter' and star of a 'pornographic' gangster movie was an incredibly nice guy with an affable and truly lovable nature. Pictures of his fight-worn face and muscular torso in the papers were simply not portraying him in the best light.

So, after much discussion, the couple decided that Alex should put the record straight by breaking his silence on their relationship. They had been seen together with the kids, as well as getting up close and personal in public, and they both felt it was now time for Alex to spill the beans.

Consequently, he gave an open interview to *new!*

magazine, in which he talked frankly and in heartfelt fashion about their flourishing relationship.

'I want to be around her all the time. I'm sad to be here now,' he joked with the journalist. 'We have an amazing connection. We spend an hour just looking at each other in the eyes, just staring at each other without talking or saying anything.'

Bravely confronting some of the media speculation head-on, he conceded that their relationship was likely to have a positive effect on his career and acknowledged that unprecedented opportunities were now coming his way. 'I wasn't even aware of how much being with Katie could help me. And it has. I understand my stock's gone up,' he admitted. 'I can't look a gift horse in the mouth as, because of our relationship, a lot more doors are going to open.'

He also set the record straight regarding the chronology of his relationships, explaining that he had split from his ex Marie before he met Katie. And in a pointed dig at Peter Andre, who had recently railed against Katie's alter ego Jordan with the comment, 'I loved Katie Price, but she left the building a long time ago,' Alex gushed, 'I love everything about her. The good, the bad and the ugly. There's no difference between Katie and Jordan.

I see her as one person. And she wants to grow. I've sort of surrendered myself to her by showing her everything about me, and she accepts me.'

He was keen to show that he was ready to settle down with the mum-of-three and was delighted to be part of her family, confirming the child-friendly attitude that best friend Sol had described. 'I love kids,' he confessed, 'and I'm really happy with Katie's family situation. When we were in the park the other day – me and the kids – that wasn't contrived. We just want to be a normal couple.'

He avoided talk of marriage, but he did have some unusual holiday plans for his girlfriend: a kung fu vacation staged high in the stunning mountains of Wudang, China. And a smitten Alex, who confided that he had never felt this way about a woman before, wasn't just planning holidays. 'I hope we have a good, long future together. It's just the right person at the right time.'

Alex also talked frankly about his cage-fighting career, and explained that he had to control his temper outside of the ring in order to keep his reputation intact. Due to Alex's martial arts skills, he himself is classed as a lethal weapon, so however much stick he might get outside of the cage, he must always be on his best behaviour. Legally, he can't get into brawls or scrapes – or he might find himself in a cage of an altogether different variety.

Luckily, Alex is a pretty calm guy, and he described himself as someone who actually thrives under pressure. Now part of one of the most-watched relationships in Britain, that was just as well. The cheeky chap pointed out that that's how diamonds are made – under pressure. 'I see myself like a diamond!' he quipped to *new!* As far as Katie Price was concerned, he was definitely her new best friend.

The bad side of fame had already reared its ugly head, but Alex's higher profile was also reaping some benefits, for instance sparking fresh interest in cage fighting, previously seen as a brutal underground sport. Suddenly, the tabloids and the men's mags were reporting on the upcoming fight between 'The Reidinator' and his next opponent, Jack 'The Stone' Mason.

The combatants were certainly happy to add fuel to the media fire. Jack, accommodatingly, vowed to 'batter' Alex and 'put him to sleep' when they met at the Ultimate Challenge UK Mayhem show on 19 September in London. And there were suggestions from the fight community that Alex's training was suffering while he followed Katie abroad and spent many well-publicized nights out with her. Would this be yet another case of a Samson destroyed by his Delilah?

Alex himself proved his fighting spirit by joining in the pre-match banter with a warning to Jack: 'I am a professional fighter and let my skills do the talking in the cage,' he told the *Daily Star*. 'My training is excellent and I feel one hundred per cent focused on the job in hand. If Jack's looking to "batter" something, then I suggest he gets a job in a fish and chip shop!'

At the offices of *Loaded*, where Katie had dropped in to talk about a photo shoot, a sports writer helpfully produced a picture of Jack 'The Stone' Mason. 'He's a big boy,' she commented with a worried tone, 'bigger than Alex.' But Katie was already making plans to support her man from the ringside at the September fight, with an entourage of no less than fifteen.

In the meantime, the charm offensive continued, with Katie pleading her case in a candid interview in the *Mirror*, during which she even offered to do a pregnancy test in front of the shocked journalist, in order to quash rumours that she was carrying Alex's child.

Telling the writer that she refused to cry on-screen, despite the public divorce, she insisted, 'I have got a great life, great kids, I enjoy my horses. I can't complain so I don't need to cry. I am not the only one that goes through divorce, it happens every day. I was clear in my head where I was going, there was no heartache to get over. I am a strong girl and I would advise every girl out there, if a man says it is over, don't go grovelling back. It is over, end of, move on.

'Pete made it very clear it was the end and he didn't want to go back. So what am I supposed to do, wait until he says I can have a boyfriend? I don't think so.'

But she was adamant that marriage and babies were not on the agenda just yet, revealing that she had even taken a pregnancy test on *What Katie Did Next* to prove to the world that she wasn't expecting. The cameras had been allowed into the bathroom and Katie and the crew had watched the test develop to a negative result together. And Katie was prepared to do the same again during the *Mirror* interview if the journalist had any doubts about her veracity – declaring that she had a test in her handbag at that very moment.

She also defended the speed at which her relationship with Alex had developed and pointed out that she hadn't instigated the divorce with Peter in the first place. But once she was single, she wasn't going to waste time or emotions by sitting at home on her own after the kids had gone to bed. That wasn't Katie's style. She was a social animal, through and through – and after all, as she so very bluntly put it, 'It is not as if I am an ugly girl and can't pull.'

She reflected briefly on the break-up with Pete, to say they had tried to make it work, having counselling and trying other supportive measures. But at the end of the day, the fairy tale was over. Nothing had worked, and the divorce was now imminent. There was no happy-ever-after for the two – even just as friends. 'I can't get near him, he won't speak to me,' Katie said, before concluding with a gentle plea for understanding from the public: 'I wasn't the one for him. But I'm not that bad, honestly.'

By this time, all communication with Peter, even when handing over the children, had stopped. The warring pair discussed the divorce through lawyers and sniped at each other in public, and Alex often bore the brunt of his girlfriend's frustration.

As the divorce date loomed, Katie felt the newspaper stories about Alex's new film were not helping her cause. She was reported to be furious having seen unedited footage of the infamous 'rape' scene. Katie was worried that the media storm would add more ammunition to Peter Andre's custody claims.

Feeling the pressure, the media-savvy model had one final card up her sleeve: an explosive revelation that would, with luck, turn the tide of public opinion in her favour – and clear Alex's name for good.

CHAPTER FOUR

FIGHTING BACK

I T WAS A secret she had carried with her since she was a struggling glamour model, finding her way in the business. The terrible revelation may never have surfaced, had Katie not felt the need to defend her man and her new relationship in the face of the ongoing criticism of Alex's controversial film, *Killer Babe*.

At the beginning of September 2009, she used her regular column in *OK!* magazine to reveal that she had been repeatedly raped as a young woman.

'I was appalled by the headlines claiming he [Alex] has taken part in something which glorifies rape,' she wrote. 'This is completely untrue. Rape is a subject very close to my heart. I was raped when I was younger, more than once.

'Needless to say, I'd never be associated with anything or anyone so sick. I've never talked about this before, but I feel I have to now because I was so hurt by these accusations that I would not take seriously a subject which affects so many women.'

She also claimed that the subject was a sensitive one for Alex, as it had affected a woman in his life. 'Someone who was close to Alex was also raped and he is as horrified as I am by these claims,' she added.

She went on to assure her readers that all was well in the relationship. 'I'm so happy at the moment,' she said. 'Alex and me are really strong. There's been a lot of rubbish written about his new gangster movie, people saying it's porn. He's acting. He didn't have sex. He had his pants on.'

And she concluded by returning to the very serious subject at the heart of her message: 'I urge any woman who has been affected by rape and needs help to talk to somebody they trust about it.'

Her piece said, Katie thought that would be that, and turned her attention back to the man she loved. Events were moving on at breakneck speed in the Price–Reid saga. Over the August bank holiday weekend, Katie got to pass Alex's toughest test: getting on with his parents.

Before the couple had met, back in July, Alex had spent most nights at home at his mum and dad's house in Aldershot, Hants. He is incredibly close to his mum, Carol, who still did his washing at that time and cooked his meals. It was therefore very important to him that the two women got on and, when his parents invited them both for a summer barbecue, he nervously introduced them.

Aware of the articles Carol and husband Bob may have read about her, and keen to make a good impression, Katie was on her best behaviour. She stayed off the booze and chatted to Alex's large family all day, complimenting Carol on the spread she had laid on in the garden of the Aldershot home. Carol later declared in the *Daily Star* that her son's new girlfriend was 'absolutely charming' and said the day was 'truly lovely, and so was the company'.

With that hurdle over, the couple concentrated on the next big event in their personal life – Katie's divorce.

On 12 August, Katie had filed divorce papers citing 'irreconcilable differences'. On 26 August, Peter counter-sued on the same grounds. The model had employed high-profile lawyer Fiona Shackleton, who famously represented Prince Charles, Madonna and Paul McCartney in their divorces. The papers were filed under the couple's real names, Katie

Price and Peter James Andrea, and showed both as petitioner and respondent.

The 'quickie' hearing eventually took place in the High Court on 8 September 2009, the twentieth of twenty-one cases that day presided over by Judge Hilary Bradley. It was all over in just 42 seconds, when she ruled the pair could 'not reasonably be expected to live together'. Both parties stated that unreasonable behaviour was ongoing, but that the dispute had not affected either's mental health.

Peter declared he had read Jordan's statement of arrangements regarding their children. But he cryptically added, 'There are several responses provided by my wife ... that are outside my knowledge to comment upon.'

On the day, neither husband nor wife attended the hearing and Peter spent the morning at *GMTV*, where he was questioned about the divorce. Host Eamonn Holmes asked the singer if he knew that the papers were going through as they spoke, and Peter replied, 'Really? Well, yeah, just before I came in, I was told that it's been accepted, yes.'

Eamonn then quipped that Peter needed to be in court and he laughed in response, 'Well, if I do, I'm in trouble because I'm here on the sofa!'

Katie, meanwhile, spent the day with the real loves of her life – her horses and her children. With the paparazzi hot on her tail, she chose to stay away from Alex and took her mind off the momentous occasion by grooming, riding and, perhaps more metaphorically, mucking out. After lunch, she was seen walking her horse in a field, accompanied by two-year-old Princess Tiaamii.

Although the divorcees had signed a pre-nuptial agreement before their lavish 2005 wedding, circumstances had changed with the birth of their two children and the amount they had earned while still wed, both apart and together, with the reality show *Katie and Peter*. The house that Katie and the children still shared in Woldingham, Surrey had been bought by both of them. Peter was adamant he didn't want any of the millions that Katie had amassed before they married, however, asking instead for a fair split of everything they had spent on the home since.

Custody issues were still being thrashed out but, despite the bitter feud between the warring pair, Katie was keen for the children to spend time with their dad and was happy for elder son Harvey, whom Pete adored, to be part of the deal.

While the former lovebirds kept quiet, Katie's ex-fiancé, Gladiator Warren Furman, aka Ace, joked about the split. 'I'm going to get in touch with Pete and ask him if he wants to join the Great Escape club with me,' he said in *The Sun*, 'because we've both had great escapes from Jordan.'

Now that the decree nisi was signed and sealed, the marriage would officially end after a six-week 'cooling off' period, designed for couples who may want to reconsider. With relations with her ex at an all-time low, and the romance with Alex going from strength to strength, a reconciliation was definitely not on the cards.

Alex, who was preparing for his big fight against Jack 'The Stone' Mason on 19 September, was relieved it was over so he could fully concentrate on his training. However, the path of true love, and Katie Price's life, seldom runs smooth and another huge storm was about to overshadow his big moment in the cage.

Two weeks after revealing her rape ordeal, Katie stirred up a further frenzy by admitting the man responsible had been, and still was, a celebrity. In an echo of the previous allegation made by presenter Ulrika Jonsson in her autobiography *Honest*, Katie refused to name the perpetrator and said she would never reveal his identity. And in a bizarre aside, published in *The Sun*, she added, 'A famous celebrity raped me, and Peter knows who it was. It was years ago, before I was with Pete, and my friends and family knew about it at the time.'

Pete, in turn, dismissed the claims that he knew about the incident and reportedly responded, 'Once again, Katie is saying things that don't make sense to me,' according to *The Sun*.

Whether Pete was taking her seriously or not, the Surrey Police certainly were. The star was contacted at her home and asked to make a formal statement about the alleged offence, which apparently took place at a London party over ten years earlier, but Katie was adamant that she would not press charges and would never name the man involved.

'No report of rape has been made,' said a police spokesman. 'Officers have spoken to her. Officers will be following lines of inquiry into this offence.'

Meanwhile, a distraught Katie was bitterly regretting her original revelation, saying in the *Mirror*, 'What's past is past and I just want to forget about it the best I can. This whole thing has been a nightmare and I wish I'd never said anything in the first place.'

As speculation continued, a former friend stepped forward to confirm that the rape had taken place. 'Everyone thinks Jordan made this whole thing up,' said the pal, who chose not to be named, speaking to the *News of the World*. 'All I can say is that she told me about the rape not long after it happened – and I believed her. She had no reason to make it up. It was a private conversation.

'She said she had gone to bed with the bloke and then things turned very, very dark. She said, "No," and that she didn't want to continue. She told me, "He just wouldn't take no for an answer." It was obvious to me that she was absolutely sincere about it all.

'She didn't want to go to the police because she didn't want to have to go through it all with strangers. I could tell she had been badly shaken up by it.

'She is resilient – she was over it by then. But she did say she shuddered whenever she saw him on TV.'

Another person who believed Katie's version of events was ex-fiancé Warren Furman, who thought he may have accused her of cheating on him with her attacker when he found the mystery man's number on her phone. When she collapsed in tears, he said, he took it as a sign of guilt.

'Seeing his name was like a red rag to a bull,' he revealed to *The Sun*. 'He had a notorious reputation in showbiz for being a serious player, a serial shagger. I screamed at her and walked out.

'But now, after hearing about her rape claim, I'm haunted by the fear that she reacted like that because of what that man had done to her.'

Although aware of the attack, Katie's mum Amy felt it was wrong of her daughter to stir things up so long after the event, as she was keen to keep her off the front pages. The whipped-up storm got completely out of Katie's control and, according to friends, she was terrified when the police began to get involved.

However, the controversy did have one positive effect, in that it cemented the friendship between Amy and Alex. The worried mum, who had been wary of the cage fighter before, saw how supportive he was throughout Katie's ordeal and was impressed by his loyalty and sensitivity.

Eventually, upset by comments from Katie's doubters, the loyal mum, who went to great lengths to stay out of the limelight herself, stepped up to defend her.

'I've known about it for years and years and years,' Amy Price told *The People*. 'Of course it has caused heartache. It was a hard decision to know what to do, but this is no publicity stunt. My daughter is so angry that people would think otherwise.'

She also revealed the extent to which the attack had affected her daughter at the time, saying Katie became 'depressed and withdrawn'. With her family around her, helping her to cope, the model slowly built up her confidence again and began to deal with the trauma she had suffered.

Amy defended her daughter's decision not to go to the police when the attack happened.

'My gut instinct at the time was perhaps she should go to the police, but at the time, would people have believed her? I don't think so. It is exactly what is happening now,' she raged. And, rightly, she cited the shocking rape prosecution success rates as being a deterrent to women reporting such crimes. All of that would have played a part in her and Katie's discussions at the time.

The loving mum showed awareness of the idea that many victims blame themselves when an attack occurs, and that some even question whether a crime has been committed. Had that been an element to her chats with Katie as she supported her daughter through her ordeal? Amy hinted that she could go into more detail about the case, but refused to do so to protect her little girl. 'My heart is saying I want to say so much, but I have Katie's feelings to think about.'

In fact, this was not the first time that Katie had revealed a sexual assault in her past. In a TV interview with Piers Morgan earlier in the year, she told how she had been sexually assaulted by a stranger in a park when she was just six years old. But she furiously denied any suggestions that she had made the new assault public to gain the sympathy vote.

'I said what I said about it in defence of Alex,' she said to the *News of the World*. 'Public sympathy is not something I look to gain from stories like this.'

As the controversy raged on, Alex was training hard for his big moment in the cage. His first major fight since becoming a bona fide celebrity was due to take place at the Ultimate Challenge UK Mayhem show at the Troxy, in east London. The mixed martial arts champion was defending his title and Katie was about to see her big, soft-hearted giant involved in a no-holds-barred fight for the very first time.

In the days leading up to the bout, despite her trauma over the divorce and the rape revelations, Katie rallied round her man, drumming up support for The Reidinator. On the night, an entourage of fifteen, including best pal Michelle Heaton, arrived at Katie's house to have a full makeover before the event.

Confident that she would be going home with a winner, Katie showed the group a top she'd ordered, which she planned to change into after the fight. Should Alex emerge victorious, she vowed to don the black, low-cut, skintight vest, which was emblazoned with 'The Champ' in sparkling rhinestones across the chest, and jump into the cage.

'I know that people want to say, "She's with a loser," but I can't go in thinking of that,' she told her pals in typically determined fashion on *What Katie Did Next*.

The evening proved tougher than expected for both the fighter and the spectator. First Alex was forced to change and warm up in the venue's kitchen, then City banker Mason proved a worthy opponent, raining blows on Alex's head and leaving a deep cut above his eye. Katie winced and hid her face behind her handbag as Alex received a battering, and was kneed in the second round.

In the final round of the three-round match, however, Alex fought back, getting a few strong blows in – and, at the final bell, The Reidinator was declared the winner.

A delighted Katie immediately stripped off to change her top and then, wearing the special vest, rewarded her conquering hero with a victory kiss – all in front of the noisy crowd.

Despite Alex's hard-fought victory, once again the papers focused on his other half – and in particular on the huge sparkling ring that she was sporting on her left hand, which sparked instant rumours that the couple had plans to tie the knot.

But pal Michelle Heaton laughed off the gossip with the statement: 'Not as far as I know – no, she's not engaged.'

Yet Michelle was not privy to the thoughts of the new champion. And as well as training for his fight, smitten Alex had been preparing a secret romantic surprise to finish off the evening.

After the fight and the customary after-party were over, and the couple were at last alone, Alex proposed to 'the love of his life'.

Without hesitation, the newly divorced glamour girl said, 'Yes.'

But a happy ending wasn't going to happen right away …

CHAPTER FIVE

JORDAN'S CROSS DRESSER

J UST BOUGHT A new black dressage horse an im calling it Jordans Cross Dresser cant wait to compete so excited.' This was Katie's post on Twitter on 31 August 2009.

In hindsight, we know the quirky name was a private joke, referring to a secret that Alex had been hiding. The burly fighter, who had always maintained that Katie knew everything about him, had clearly confessed his most private fetish to his new love. But nothing in Katie's life stays hidden for long and, a month after the naming of the new horse, Alex was at the centre of another media storm when the papers claimed to have uncovered his secret – that he liked to dress in women's clothes and call himself Roxanne.

The revelation, which appeared to have started spreading after Katie flashed pictures of her lover in drag at Simon Cowell's birthday party, was leaked to the press in early October. 'A friend' also claimed that the model was fine with the idea of her lover dressing up and had even bought him a pair of high heels.

However, the revelations of his penchant for miniskirts and fishnets initially threatened to drive a wedge between the two, as contradictory statements began to be issued from both camps.

At first, Alex's friends declared that Katie had made the story up for fun and complained that Alex was being made a laughing stock in the fighting community. There were even fears that Katie was deliberately trying to make him look like 'a freak' because she was preparing to dump him. *The Sun* claimed that Reid's spokesman told them, 'This is Katie messing around. It looks really sleazy and is incredibly frustrating for Alex. This has made Alex question what sort of woman he's with. He feels he's being used as a pawn in her game to get rich and famous.

'She is off plugging her books everywhere and now she's making up ludicrous stories about Alex to get even more publicity. He doesn't know how long he can take it.'

Katie's friends, however, were reportedly telling

the same paper, 'I understand Alex has dressed up as a woman. Roxanne is the name he uses, like Barry Humphries uses Dame Edna Everage. There's a shock element to it, but Katie lives with it.'

Soon pictures of Alex in drag were doing the rounds, although the first to emerge were from a fancy-dress event some five years before, when he had attended the School Disco night at the Hammersmith Palais with a group of other fighters.

Alex himself was staying tight-lipped on the subject – but those close to him were making matters worse with further revelations.

Ex-lover Danielle Sims claimed he had called her in the middle of the night and voiced his fears over Katie's manipulation of the controversy. She told *The Sun* he had whispered, 'Katie's stitching me up. She told the papers I'm a cross-dresser to make me look like a freak. I'm sure she did it so that when she dumps me, people won't blame her. We've been arguing a lot and I'm sure she's about to dump me. She's had enough of me and is already getting in the cheap shots.'

In an exclusive interview with the *Sunday Mirror*, Danielle also asserted that Alex had been dressing up in women's clothing since he was a teenager, and that she once walked in on him in full drag during their relationship.

'I looked around his bedroom and saw a woman. I thought, "Who the hell are you?" It wasn't until "she" said, "Hello" that I realized it was Alex. He was sat there in stockings, a dress with a basque underneath, a wig on his head. And he was very expertly, slowly, painting his nails.

'I just stood there for what seemed like an eternity. I was in total, utter shock.'

She revealed that the dressing-up usually happened after the stress of a big fight, as a way to relieve the tension after the intense training of the build-up. 'There's probably lots of men who do this, but never talk about it. I don't think it's anything to be embarrassed about and it certainly doesn't make him any less of a man.'

And she was sure that this other side to Alex would not put off the open-minded glamour girl in the long run.

'I'm sure they'll marry next year. Alex wants kids and marriage, he's old-fashioned like that. I know he'll love those kids of hers. Despite what happened at the Simon Cowell party, I think Katie is quite secure in him dressing up and that's great for them.

She probably handles it better than I did. I actually think they're great together.'

Katie certainly seemed to be taking it in her stride and, in private, she was urging him to come clean about the skeletons in his closet. Well aware that the hungry press are like a dog with a bone once they get hold of a juicy story, she was sure that there would be more and more digging until he revealed all.

While many women would have run a mile when faced with this situation, Katie understood, perhaps better than anyone, what living with an alter ego is like. Having switched between the wildly different personalities of Katie Price and Jordan since becoming a teenage model, Katie sympathized with the desire to escape into another persona. Her playful nature meant she even encouraged the foible, taking snaps of 'Roxanne' and finding clothes for Alex to wear. Yet again, she chose to stand by her man.

A few days after the cross-dressing story broke, Katie quashed rumours of a split with a brief statement, reading, 'We are very much together.'

In a later report, after her reappearance on *I'm a Celebrity ... Get Me Out of Here!*, Katie revealed that Alex had confessed to his cross-dressing very early on in their relationship – and she had immediately insisted that he dress up.

'Did I have sex with Alex while he was dressed as a woman? Of course!' she allegedly said on a censored out-take from the jungle programme, which was later reported in the *News of the World*. 'He told me about it the second day I knew him and I thought he was mucking about. He doesn't go around dressed like it – it's only a sexual thing. I don't judge what people do. Alex says, "I'm an actor." He just lives it as a pure sexual thing. When he told me the first time, I did him up myself. I said, "Get up to my dressing room and let me put your make-up on!"

'It's really surreal to have your boyfriend dressing up in your stuff. Interesting, isn't it? I think more people should talk about it, really. Nobody knows what goes on behind those doors. He's not hurting anyone. I think it's nice if people are different and unique.'

Even Peter, it seemed, accepted the latest news with grace, asking only that the children were not involved. 'Whatever people are doing in their private lives, and that goes for them or anyone, can you please not do it in front of the kids,' he said to

The Sun. 'I'm not going to criticize, I'm not going to say, "How dare you do this or that," just don't do it in front of the kids. Give me that little bit of respect.'

Finally, under pressure from Katie, Alex decided to spill the beans and reveal all, giving a no-holds-barred interview to *OK!* magazine about the rumours.

'It's a bit of fun. I've dressed up as a woman and it's a laugh,' he admitted to the mag. 'I've got nothing to hide and I'm proud of who I am. If I go out and wear a dress, so f***ing what? I don't want a sex change.'

But the cross-dressing, he insisted, had not had a damaging effect on his relationship. 'There's a big attraction between us. I love her so much it's ridiculous,' he said.

And Katie backed that up by confirming that, after Alex's first confession, she had made him dress up for more fun in the bedroom. 'The outfit changes, the make-up, hair, the lot. And I boss him about. Before Alex met me, he hadn't dressed up for a year. And when he told me, I was like, "Oh my God, I've got to dress you up,"' she told Graham Norton on *The Graham Norton Show*. 'So I dress him – the wigs, eyelashes, everything. And at first he was like,

"This is a bit weird, I'm not used to a girl doing me up." Call me strange, call me weird, whatever – but I love it.'

And after revealing that Alex had lost a nipple after using a clamp on it, she bragged, 'You name it, he's been there, done it. He says he's try-sexual [he'll try anything once] – I've never been with anyone so adventurous. Anything goes with him. I'm having such a fun time.'

Defiant as ever, Katie was determined to have some more fun with the other woman in her lover's life, and what better occasion than Halloween? As Peter was pictured in Shoreham, near Brighton, taking Junior and Princess to a kids' party (with the kids dressed as Woody from *Toy Story* and as a cute red devil), Katie was snapped at the Bloodlust Ball at Hampton Court House in London.

While she, as usual, left little to the imagination with a skintight Catwoman outfit and stockings, Alex also played up to the cameras ... in lingerie, stockings and full make-up. His fishnet bodice revealed a black bra and panties, and he finished off the look with thigh-high patent leather boots. With his bulging biceps and sportsman's thighs, the result was hardly feminine, but it had the desired effect of turning the tables on the press and having a laugh on his own terms.

Later, however, when his popularity reached its peak after he won *Celebrity Big Brother*, Alex tried to bury the public fixation with 'Roxanne'. He commented to *Star* magazine in February 2010: 'Cross-dressing is only one per cent of Alex Reid. Big deal. I hope I can move away from it now.'

But in autumn 2009, the issue was red hot. Nevertheless, even as the cross-dressing controversy raged, Katie had her mind on other things. At the end of October, her marriage was finally ended when the decree absolute was issued by the High Court. The clearly emotional model marked the occasion by adding fuel to the feud with her ex-husband – and turning on his manager and friend Claire Powell.

Businesswoman Claire had once looked after both Katie and Peter's affairs. However, in the wake of the split, she had continued to work with Pete, but she and Katie had parted ways. Furious that her former manager had chosen Peter after the break-up, Katie had in fact sparked a row weeks before when she had called Claire 'that devil woman' and ordered her lawyers to pick the children up from Pete's after he left them in her care. With the four-year marriage officially over, Katie now accused her of being the real reason for the divorce.

'The trouble is, before, I felt married to two people – Pete and our management. And it was like Pete was married to two women, Claire and me. And it just suffocated me,' she told *Now*. 'If I'm going to blame anyone for the end of my relationship with Pete, I'd have to lay some of the blame with Claire.'

Angry Claire, who has been credited with much of Katie's lucrative transformation from topless model to millionaire businesswoman, immediately denied any wrongdoing and threatened to sue over the comments. 'She has to find someone to blame for the marriage break-up. I am not that person,' she said in *The Sun*.

Increasingly annoyed that both the press and public were still siding with her ex, Katie posted a series of comments about 'nice guy' Peter on Twitter. One accused him of threatening to break Alex's legs in a phone row and another pleaded with her fans not to believe the papers' version of events. 'Alex is calm a real gentle guy stop believing what you read an realise pete is not the sweet guy that he always portrays,' she wrote.

Despite friends' fears that she was not coping

well with the divorce, and was jeopardizing her relationship with Alex as a result, Katie insisted in the *Daily Star* that she was past caring for her ex. 'I am over it. One hundred per cent. I'm so into Alex. It was over even before Pete and I [officially] split up.'

What Katie did next, then, proved a shock to fans and family alike. At the beginning of November, after long negotiations with ITV and endless discussions with Alex, she announced that the rumours were true – she was returning to the very jungle where she had met her ex-husband, thus becoming the first contestant ever to return to *I'm a Celebrity... Get Me Out of Here!*

CHAPTER SIX

FAIRY-TALE ENDING

In the wake of Katie's split from Peter Andre, she hit
the club scene in Ibiza in jaw-dropping fashion.

A shot of Katie in Ibiza in a pensive mood, suggesting that her divorce is far from plain sailing.

Left: New couple Katie and Peter at an *I'm a Celebrity* party in 2004.

Below: After running the London Marathon in 2009 – just days after Katie's miscarriage, and two weeks before the couple split up.

Right: The divorce means Katie and Peter now share custody: here Katie drops off Princess Tiaamii and Junior at Pete's house.

Above: Katie and Alex on the night they met – 19 July 2009.

Below: This saucy pic of the two on holiday in Marbella caused a storm of controversy.

Left: A now famous shot of the couple kissing on a summer's day in Brighton.

Below: The chemistry is clear to see at a polo match in Spain.

Right: Alex, Katie and Harvey on a family day out to Thorpe Park.

Left: Alex and Junior having fun in Brighton.

Above: One of the family: Alex, Katie and her brother Daniel at a charity run for Cancer Research.

Right: Katie celebrates Alex's win in a cage fight with a trademark show-stopping outfit.

Overleaf: Alex Reid: champion.

O N REFLECTION, THE apparent shock decision to return to the challenging TV show was all too easy to understand. Towards the end of October, the public backlash against Katie had begun to take extreme forms. The distressed model was convinced she and Alex had become 'the most hated couple in Britain'. She had been verbally abused by crowds outside London venues where she had attended parties, and had even been called vile names at the September fight when she had gone to support Alex.

On 9 October, she learned that Peter had won the ratings battle, too, trouncing her reality show *What Katie Did Next* with his own series *Peter Andre: The Next Chapter*, which pulled in 1.44 million viewers as opposed to her 1.28 million.

But the antagonism towards the star took a very sinister turn when a crank sent four letters threatening to harm her horses. Another used a martial arts site to post a similar threat, seemingly over her appearance at Alex's cage fight.

Terrified, Katie called in police when she received the letters, which branded her a 'slag' and a 'hoar' [sic] and vowed to slash her beloved animals. They were assembled from letters cut from a newspaper and one was signed 'Team Andre'.

The separate threat, posted on a mixed martial arts (MMA) forum, referred to her 'Champ' vest and warned, 'Don't wear the T-shirt again or the horses will be killed.' Katie was so shaken by the threats that she laid on extra security for her book-signing trip to Dublin and apparently suffered a panic attack while at the event.

'She was in tears about the threats,' said a friend to the *News of the World*. 'She can't understand why someone would be so evil. She got very anxious on Friday. It was basically a panic attack. She needed to sit down and be comforted by friends. She can understand why people might not like her, but to call her all those evil names and threaten innocent animals is disgusting.'

The four hugely valuable horses, Cross Dresser, Glamour Girl, Blaze and Dana – who was a thirtieth birthday gift from Pete – were safe in the super-secure Haywards Heath stables run by Katie's dressage trainer Andrew Gould. But Katie was clearly upset and used her Twitter page to plead with her 'haters' to leave her family, animals and even her ex-husband alone.

'dont attack my children, family, friends, horses and pete but you can attack me its fine go ahead i can take it but dont attack them thanksxx' she tweeted on 1 November. A few minutes later, she added, 'come on all you people who slag me off an hate me get it off your chest but then give someone a compliment an make someones day :)'

She followed this with another invitation for her enemies, posting, 'come on haters attack me! your right, im always wrong im hated i never do anything right do i sorry for that!! Xx' and 'your all asking why hate me!! you obviously think ive done alot wrong so give me what you think i deserve then leave me be pleasexx.'

The tone was increasingly desperate. Since splitting from Pete in May, Katie had been through hell. It especially distressed her that she had become the villain of the piece, even though it was Pete's decision to end the marriage. She had coped with the tide turning against her with her usual defiant mantra – 'I don't care what they think. My family and my fans love me' – but the threat to her horses was the final straw.

Although the sick prankster who posted the online threat was later caught, the sender of the letters has not yet been traced at the time of writing.

At the beginning of November, Katie was officially hailed a witch in a small Kentish town. The organizers of the popular Edenbridge bonfire, which burns an effigy of someone in the public eye each year, chose the glamour girl as the 2009 subject. The 27-foot guy, modelled on Jordan, wore a pink top, jodhpurs and riding boots, and had a bundle of newspapers in one hand and the heads of Peter Andre and Alex in the other. Thousands watched as she was burnt at the stake, following in the charred footsteps of Russell Brand, Tony Blair and even Saddam Hussein.

At the same time, Alex was suffering from the public lashing in his own way. The MMA websites were full of insults for the fighter, and he admitted things had turned nasty at the September showdown with Jack Mason.

'Take my last fight. There were a lot of haters

I had to deal with,' he said to the *Daily Star*. 'As I left the cage, several people tried to throw punches at me and even break into my dressing room. If it wasn't for my own guys being with me, who knows what would have happened?'

Although Alex had gone along with the media frenzy surrounding his cross-dressing habit, and had poked fun at himself with his outrageous Halloween outfit, he was privately worried that he was not being taken seriously in the tough world of cage fighting. His high-profile relationship was costing him his hardman reputation and he felt it was time to get his head back in the game.

'For now, I'm keeping myself to myself and concentrating on my training. To all my critics who want to slag me off, it just fires me up to train harder. A lot of people are saying I'm bringing the UK MMA scene into disrepute. But what I do outside of the fight scene is my business. The last few months have been a crazy rollercoaster.'

As Katie contemplated her future, and how to turn the tide of public opinion in her favour, ITV decided to make her an amazing offer. The producers of *I'm a Celebrity ... Get Me Out of Here!* had been closely watching the dramatic story of their first married couple unfold and they knew that a reappearance from Katie would be ratings gold. The millions of viewers who had watched her meet and fall in love with Pete would lap up the chance to see how she coped with a return to the same jungle without him.

Equally, they must have known that in the pantomime of her life, she was currently painted as the villain. Those who loved to hate her would be voting in droves to see her suffer in the grisly Bushtucker Trials – thus not only bringing in hard cash for the production, but also generating a whole new drama in the jungle.

The decision was a no-brainer. According to unconfirmed reports, the eager bosses offered Katie a massive £350,000 fee to return.

The glamour model and mum-of-three had some serious thinking to do. At first, her gut reaction was to say no. Her mind was in turmoil as she mulled the offer over, and she told her circle of friends that she was not going to accept. Having worked hard to get over her split with Pete, she felt being in the place where they had met and enjoyed such an intense experience together would stir up memories and feelings she would rather forget.

On deeper reflection, however, she began to change

her mind. She was desperate to remind the public of the real Katie Price, and return to the popularity she had enjoyed when she left the jungle the first time, hand in hand with her new love. Perhaps, if viewers saw her accepting the challenges with the same amount of guts and determination as she had shown the first time round, she would earn renewed respect.

There was also the issue of closure. Despite her defiant persona and frequent verbal swipes at her ex, Katie was struggling with the pain of the divorce and the war of words that had sprung up between her and Pete. Even her love for Alex was being tainted by the bitterness caused by the split. Twice, in October and early November, it was reported that Katie had asked Alex to move out of her home for a few days, to give her some space. She was having trouble moving on, and began to think that a return to the jungle might finally lay those ghosts to rest.

All in all, the offer began to seem more and more attractive. The opportunities it afforded were unquestionably unique and as Katie weighed up the pros and cons, she found herself unexpectedly warming to the idea.

As she contemplated this next huge step in her

career, a sudden illness in the family brought Peter and Katie together for the first time in months. At the beginning of November, Harvey was admitted to hospital with suspected swine flu – a potentially life-threatening illness, particularly for children with 'underlying health issues', such as his.

Katie was 'frantic' when the seven-year-old failed to keep down his food, had trouble breathing and his temperature soared to alarming levels. The worried mum cancelled book signings at Northampton and Milton Keynes, while Harvey's stepdad pulled out of turning on the Christmas lights at a London store to rush to his side.

Harvey was kept in for 48 hours, before being discharged into Katie's care. The awkward reunion between his parents, while far from healing all wounds, put a new light on the bitter relationship between the exes.

'This has brought everything back to reality and put all the petty fighting into perspective,' said Katie later to the *Daily Star*. She was relieved that they had managed to be civil to each other for the sake of the little boy.

After nearly a fortnight at home, seeing little of Alex as she nursed her sick son back to health, Katie prepared to fly to Australia, her decision made. The cage fighter's absence from the house had inevitably sparked rumours of a rift between the couple, but Katie was quick to deny them.

'I'm very happy in the relationship I'm in,' she told *The Sun*. She also explained her decision to return to the survival show, saying, 'I want closure on the fairy tale that I had. I'm definitely not going into that jungle looking for love.'

Meanwhile, in the *Mirror*, she once again took the chance to dismiss rumours of a split from Alex, with the simple comment, 'I can't wait to spend more time together.'

Having finally agreed to the TV deal, Katie was to be the *I'm a Celebrity* secret weapon, but the big gun had already claimed its first casualty – her annoyed ex Peter Andre. The singer had landed a lucrative contract to provide behind-the-scenes coverage of the jungle programme direct from Australia for ITV's magazine show, *This Morning*. When he discovered his ex was flying in, Pete was forced to pull out, explaining that he couldn't be expected to provide unbiased commentary on his former wife's antics. He also felt he needed to be at home to look after the children while their mum was on the other side of the world.

The camp began on 15 November without any appearance from Katie. The stars of the show were *Strictly Come Dancing* professional dancer Camilla Dallerup (who was later replaced by boxer Joe Bugner, after Camilla quit for health reasons), clean queen Kim Woodburn, actress Lucy Benjamin, interior designers – and partners – Justin Ryan and Colin McAllister, American actor George Hamilton, *Hollyoaks* star Stuart Manning, chef Gino D'Acampo, singer Sabrina Washington, snooker player Jimmy White and former Page Three girl Samantha Fox.

When asked about the possibility of Katie Price joining them in the jungle, the reaction was less than favourable from her fellow celebs. Interior designer Colin claimed that she had once been rude to him and partner Justin at a red carpet do in LA.

'We tried to chat to Jordan and she was really, really, really unpleasant in her refusal to do an interview,' he commented to the *Daily Star* before flying into the jungle. 'I'd be disappointed if she was in there. I mean, what is she actually famous for? We'd rather her boyfriend Alex Reid was in there than her. We are loving the whole trannie thing he has going on. But underneath it all he is hot.'

Italian chef Gino D'Acampo said he preferred

Peter because 'he is a great guy'. 'As for Jordan, as a businesswoman she is very clever,' he continued to the same paper. 'I take my hat off to anyone who can make a career with a pair of boobs. But as a mum or a woman – I am not gonna comment. I don't agree on many things she does.'

Dancer Camilla, who admitted to being 'scared' of the model, chipped in, 'I am very much Team Pete. He is a lovely guy. As for Jordan, I think she can be a handful.'

As her fellow contestants settled into camp and claimed their hammocks, Katie was in Los Angeles, preparing for the upcoming ordeal as only Katie would: by having a Botox treatment and some new hair extensions.

Surrounded by friends, she was optimistic about the experience she was about to embark upon, feeling that the real Katie Price would shine through on the show. She posted a farewell to fans on her Twitter site, using the famous catchphrase that has become familiar to her reality-show followers, 'Never underestimate the pricey !! Another journey begins lol xxxx.'

This journey was going to prove a lot bumpier than she had imagined.

CHAPTER SEVEN

TRIALS AND TRIBULATIONS

As his feisty woman was flying to the Gold Coast of Australia to take on one of the biggest challenges of her life, Alex had a TV triumph of his own to celebrate. The fame he had won through the relationship with Katie was finally paying off, and Alex had landed himself a TV deal. *Alex Reid: The Fight of His Life*, which was to air on Bravo, would see the fighter learning new combat skills, including one scrapping style known as 'drunken fighting', as well as following his training for the spring fight against Tom 'Kong' Watson.

'I'm over the moon to be doing what I love most,' he commented to the *Daily Star*.

But for the next few weeks, all eyes would be on Katie and her return to the jungle where she had met her ex-husband six years before. Katie was booked to enter the camp a day later than the ten original celebrities, who were not looking forward to her arrival.

Justin dismissed her as a 'cold, hard, manipulative woman who just charges ahead grabbing every opportunity', and his partner Colin joked, 'Why would someone want to come back? If Dorothy wanted to go back to Oz, I'd say, "Maybe there are other things you should be doing."' Gino declared he would rather share camp room with Peter, and few of the other campers had a kind word to say about her.

Back at the six-star Palazzo Versace Hotel in Brisbane, where Katie was gearing up for her dramatic entrance, she was reflecting on the difference between the Jordan of six years before and the Katie Price of today.

'Who am I? I'm trouble,' she laughed, during a pre-jungle interview for the show. 'I'm Katie Price aka Jordan. Six years ago, I would have said, "I'm Jordan, but my real name is Katie Price." On the back of my shirt last time it said Jordan, but this time it says Katie. It's a bit weird, really.'

In fact, it went to show how far she had come since her first stint on *I'm a Celebrity*. Back in 2004, she was the best-known glamour girl in Britain – but still 'only' a glamour girl, and one who used an alter ego at that. Now, she was practically a walking industry, with a vast range of branded merchandise, and her real name was used more frequently than the pseudonym that had made her famous.

But with that recognition came a problem. When it was Jordan making headlines, there was an understanding that it wasn't 'the real Katie Price'. But Katie herself was in the limelight now, and the past few months had seen her come under some heavy criticism. Could she turn that around? There was no alter ego to turn to now. This was Katie Price, pure and simple.

Asked why she felt she wanted to go back on the show, she joked during the interview, 'Because I've got "mad" written across my forehead.'

But then she continued, in all seriousness, 'For the other people going in there, it's a game show, but for me, it's like closure.

'I'm going back into a place where a big fairy tale began for me. I met my husband in there, I've had two more beautiful children from that experience. Last time, from the moment I woke up to the moment I went to sleep, it was "Pete, Pete, Pete". And it was still "Pete, Pete, Pete" when I came out of the jungle, until he came out.'

This time, her experience on the show would be completely different. No Pete. No romance. She was coming in as an outsider – and an unpopular one at that. But Katie was pleased about the novelty, saying, 'It's a new chapter for me, it's closure and I want to enjoy the whole experience.'

One of the key motivations for Katie in re-entering the jungle was the chance to show the public what she was made of, and to remind them what the real Katie Price was truly like. She was sick of being the panto villain and the target of vicious negative publicity. Here was an opportunity to redress the balance and hopefully turn the tide of public favour in her direction. Clearly mindful of how she wanted to come across to the viewers, she said, 'I think people will see that I'm really down to earth and rounded. I'm nowhere near having a breakdown; I'm not nuts. I'm actually quite normal.'

For many celebs going into the jungle, some of their greatest concerns focus on the personal grooming facilities. Here there were no complimentary bath oils or Molton Brown toiletries, nor pristine white cotton towels. For the next three weeks, good old Mother Nature made up bedroom, bathroom and dressing room, all in one. Perhaps unsurprisingly, image-conscious Katie's beauty routine seemed to be on her mind as she prepared to go make-up free for the three-week duration of the show. She asked that her luxury item be make-up artist Gary ... but she didn't get away with it. Her face would be au naturel for the weeks ahead. Katie didn't seem to mind too much, though, quipping, 'At least I've got Botox this time!'

Her love of glamour was shared by her daughter, she revealed to the *Mirror* in an interview ahead of her jungle entrance: 'Princess is a mini-me. She's a really girly girl who loves sparkly things and having her nails done. She has naturally curly blonde hair, which I straightened recently and it didn't look good – she looked like a little troll.'

Very soon, Princess might not be the only one. Knowing all too well the lack of decent washing facilities in the jungle, Katie was particularly worried about how her new hair extensions would cope during the challenge ahead, and feared they would get matted in the river water.

She also revealed that she had asked for a knife and fork if she had to eat anything chewy in a Bushtucker Trial because of concerns about what the jungle grubs and animal parts might do to the veneers on her teeth.

But these were all creature comforts, really – non-essential, superficial worries that were a minor inconvenience. Nonetheless, the pre-show interview concluded with a glimpse of a rare sight: a vulnerable Katie. Just before entering the jungle, she begged, 'Please don't hurt me too much.'

If the plea was meant for the voting public, it fell on deaf ears. Katie was about to endure one of the most traumatic and torturous weeks of her life, at the cruel hands of the British viewers.

Katie's trials began before she even met her fellow contestants. As she entered the jungle, in the wild Springbrook National Park, she found a note pinned to a tree beside a stagnant pool of fish guts and cockroaches. Before she joined the others, she was told, she would have to unclip twelve floating yellow balls from the pool and put them into a basket, in order to win treats for the camp.

Her intense phobia of water, combined with the vile smell of rotting fish, made this a tough challenge. 'I'm not good with water, and I can't tell you how much it stinks,' she complained. After putting her head under in the rancid-smelling pool, she gagged and hyperventilated – before carrying on. 'I couldn't see anything. It was revolting, it was disgusting,

I had a panic attack,' she revealed. 'But I realized I had to do it for the others.'

After emerging with seven stars and triumphantly choosing gifts of tea, coffee, sugar and chocolate, she beamed and said, 'They're going to love me.' But the inevitable twist in the tale meant that her campmates would have to give up their luxury items if she decided they should have the gifts, which she did.

Despite their earlier comments, the contestants greeted the new arrival with open arms and showbiz kisses. And she instantly apologized to Justin and Colin for the snub in LA.

As Katie settled in, her straight-talking charm began to win the campers round and many of them seemed to be warming to her. But the public were determined to put her through the mill while they were in control, and Katie found herself chosen for the dreaded Bushtucker Trials at the earliest opportunity.

For her first trial, Katie had to confront her three biggest fears: spiders, being underwater and claustrophobia. The Deathly Burrows challenge saw her crawl into a network of tunnels filled with frogs, spiders and beetles. As she slowly crawled through the tiny spaces, she told herself, 'Nothing's gonna kill you.' But the mantra didn't make the challenge any easier, and the knowledge that the tunnels would soon be filled with water filled her with dread.

Battling her fears, Katie managed to collect four stars before the tunnel was suddenly flooded with gushing water, at which point she suffered a massive panic attack. The rangers rushed to pull her out of the trial; shaking and gasping for breath, it was several moments before she could speak to hosts Ant and Dec.

Yet her bravery didn't cut any ice with the watching public. The following day, the unforgiving viewers had more in store for the former Page Three girl. Her second trial saw her sealed in a revolving bottle with 60,000 cockroaches, worms and other creepy-crawlies for company, while she answered questions on Australia. For each question answered correctly, she could unscrew a cork star, and she managed to bag six.

Crawling out of the bottle, covered in critters, Katie immediately stripped off her top, declaring with characteristic bluntness, 'I've gotta get my tits out, I don't care.'

'We're not complaining,' joked Ant McPartlin.

Katie then went back to the camp with her six stars, half of those on offer.

Away from the trials, Katie was making friends. In particular, she was getting on well with former EastEnder Lucy Benjamin and Italian chef Gino D'Acampo. In a quiet moment, Gino asked her why she thought she got such bad press, and she replied that she felt it was all about the split from Peter.

'The last seven months, they wanted a good cop and a bad cop,' she explained. 'I don't believe what I read in the papers and I take it on the chin. It makes me so strong. It's like I have a sheet [in front of me] and they can fire bullets, but they won't get through.'

But she was at pains to point out that her tough exterior hid a soppier side, which only came out in her private life.

'Take me away from the industry and I'm such a soft girl,' she told him. 'I'm quite needy. I want cuddles all the time, I want to be told: "I love you." But when it comes to business and media, I'm so hard.'

In reply to a question about why her marriage had failed, she said, 'Lots of reasons. Insecurities on both sides.'

If ever Katie was in need of a cuddle it was the following day, when she found out that she had been nominated for her third trial, Jungle School. As Ant and Dec read out her name, she covered her eyes and began shaking visibly, terrified of the ordeal that lay ahead, and rare tears sprang into her eyes. She stood up next to Ant and Dec and her voice broke as she said, 'If you're watching, kids, I love you.'

Then she pulled herself together and declared, 'I'm the huntsman. I've got to get the food.'

Watched by the rest of the group for the first time, Katie put her face in slimy mealworm pupae, then writhing worms; retrieved cardboard words from a sphere of snakes; attempted to catch an eel; and was finally placed in a plastic coat and hat filled with cockroaches.

'I'm glad the group were there to watch me so they can see what I have to do for the food,' she admitted afterwards. 'But they were probably disappointed as well because I'm sure they would like to do a challenge.'

With nine out of twelve stars under her belt, she had earned the camp's dinner, but, more importantly, she had earned the gratitude and respect of her fellow contestants. Her panic before the trial, and her determination to go through with it, had won a few new members for Team Price.

'Trust me, this was not for the cameras,' said Jimmy White in the Bush Telegraph. 'She was shaking with fear. She's so brave, I call her the Ranger Girl.'

'Katie is incredible,' marvelled Colin. 'One minute she's shaking, she's so scared, with tears in her eyes, and then, all of a sudden, the shutters come down and she's like Ironman – impenetrable.'

And Gino joined in the praise with, 'Who would not be proud of a woman who could do such a thing? It's incredible, just incredible.'

One seemingly sympathetic star, however, was not as easily won over. After Katie, perhaps naively, asked her campmates if she was what they had expected, celebrity cleaner Kim Woodburn launched into a tirade against the model and branded her a 'publicity seeker'.

'You're a publicity seeker and you do it well,' she ranted, as the others looked on in shocked silence. 'You protest about it, but you love it. You've come into the jungle twice and you have twelve million viewers, and you wouldn't have it any other way.

You've got a lovely body. Make as much money as you can. But don't pretend you hate it – you love it, dear.

'For some reason, you fascinate the papers, so go for it, but don't pretend you're not causing a lot of it – you're causing it all. You love it, so stop your nonsense.'

Stunned Katie replied, 'We're all talented in our own way, Kim,' while Lucy and Gino shifted awkwardly beside Kim.

'I found that really uncomfortable,' said Lucy later. 'If it had been me, I would have been mortified, but Katie is a law unto herself. She just shrugs and says, "I make you right."'

And new pal Gino was impressed by her handling of the outburst. 'This probably isn't the last time that Katie is going to get an attack like that, but what she does is great,' he said. 'She smiles, she agrees most of the time, and moves on. She must be used to that sort of thing.'

But Katie, who later joked, 'She battered me,' had more worrying things to contend with than a disgruntled cleaning lady. The thought of doing another trial lay heavy on her mind, and the cracks were beginning to show.

'I've had enough,' she told the camera. 'I miss my children, I'm hungry, I want a nice bed. I'm absolutely ready to leave camp. I don't want to have to put myself through these horrible challenges. I don't like it.'

Then she told the group, 'I've just said I'm going home. I can't take it any more.'

Jimmy persuaded her to stay, with the words, 'You're winning in more ways than one. You're getting the food and doing the trials. They're not beating you, you're beating them.'

And Gino pleaded with the public, 'Everybody is voting for her to do these trials, but it's not fair. Other people want to have a go and it's not fair on Katie – every time she has to go through all that. What's the point?'

Katie admitted that just the thought of being picked again sent her into a panic attack. 'I don't need it,' she fretted. 'I started panicking, thinking it's going to be me. I was thinking, "Not again," because it's live and the pressure. I think the public want to give me a bad time. You can't take it personally, though it's hard not to. They've seen me battered for the last three or four days. Let someone else have a go.'

After hearing she had been voted to face a fourth ordeal, Katie begged, 'Oh please, please, I can't do it any more.

'Can you believe that? Why do they keep voting for me?' she asked.

Back at home, a devoted Alex was biting his nails every night and hoping that Katie would escape the Bushtucker Trials, while her family was beginning to get seriously worried. Asked by the *Mirror* what it was like to watch her daughter suffering on live TV, mum Amy admitted, 'It's painful, but we told her, "You know you're going to get every trial." They're taking out their spite on her. It's like the gladiators. It's like, "Let's stone them."'

Appearing on ITV show *This Morning*, Katie's brother Daniel Price, known as Danny, said, 'She loves going into the jungle, she loves the challenges. I don't think it's a bad thing for her, but the trials are mentally very, very tough.'

Yet again Katie conquered her fears in order to feed the contestants, who were now split into two camps. Panting and urging herself on, she climbed a sheer, 60-foot rock face by sticking her hands in 'Hell Holes', which were occupied by a variety of creatures. She coped admirably with rats and lizards, but freaked out when forced to thrust her hand inside holes full of spiders and snakes, all the time hyperventilating and screaming, 'I'm petrified! I'm gonna die!'

Coming down from the 'Rocky Horror' with nine out of twelve stars, she predicted, 'I reckon I'm going to do the rest of them.'

'Do you think you're being punished for something?' asked Declan Donnelly.

'Probably,' replied Katie. 'I am the baddie, but I am a good person really. I'm loving it in camp and the more I'm there, the more banter there is and the more cheeky I'm getting.'

That wasn't always true. For as well as enduring the Bushtucker Trials, Katie was dealing with an emotional rollercoaster caused by the memories of her first time in the jungle, namely meeting and getting to know her future husband. She was sleeping in the same hammock she had been in before and everywhere she looked she was reminded of her love for him. Inevitably, Pete was the subject of many of her conversations, but, perhaps deliberately, Alex was hardly mentioned.

On one occasion, Katie was asked if she would like to be friends with her ex.

'I'd love that,' she replied. 'If I had it my way, I'd still have Pete, eventually, when he comes round, to come up, you know, when the kids have birthday parties … us both be there. It's nice for the kids to have both their parents and both get on.'

Back in England, unsurprisingly, Alex was pining and admitted to feeling 'sad and lonely'. Yet he was also bursting with pride at the courage shown by his feisty girlfriend.

'When she got nine stars on Friday night's show, I swelled with pride,' he told the *News of the World*. 'That's my girl. It's the real her. She's been very brave. It pisses me off when people go around saying those panic attacks are fake. I know for a fact she has problems with enclosed spaces and especially water, so she did the best she could.

'I've also been so struck by her bravery in the challenges and her intelligence. When she spelt "kangaroo" backwards so quickly, I was so impressed. I knew I was madly in love with her before she went in there, but now I know this is the woman I have to be with forever.'

And lovestruck Alex was particularly pleased at the way his girlfriend was coming across on the programme. Aware that Katie had been partly motivated to return to the jungle to show the public the real her, he was delighted that her true personality was shining through, saying, 'People are starting to see she's not this home-wrecking nasty woman who's selfish and can't relate to anyone. She's dealing with the people in there really well.'

The following day, as predicted, Katie was voted for a fifth trial, named Vile Vending, alongside Kim Woodburn. The eating challenge saw Katie cope with bugs, witchetty grubs and even a kangaroo's anus, but she refused to munch on the animal's testicle, a mainstay of the Bushtucker Trials.

Despite her determination, however, after being voted in for a sixth trial, the distraught star was teetering close to the edge of a breakdown.

As a worried Alex made plans to fly out to Australia to be with her when she left the jungle, Michelle Heaton, who was already on hand in Oz, revealed how fragile her best friend had become. The heartless treatment of the British public, and the thought of taking part in another ordeal, were taking a huge toll on Katie's mental health.

In a message passed to Michelle through the show's producers, which was later published in *The People*, Katie told her pal, 'I never realized quite how cruel the great British public could be. I'm really worried if it carries on like this I'll end up cracking up. I'm really tired, I'm exhausted. I am doing everything I can, I have come on this show, I've bared everything and been completely myself. If that isn't going to get me any kind of acceptance, then I don't know what I can do.'

Michelle admitted that she was frightened her pal would be unable to cope, but said she was sure she wouldn't walk out of the show. Nonetheless, she was worried for her.

All too aware that Katie's popularity had taken an extreme nosedive since her divorce, Michelle seemed hopeful that Katie had managed, at least in part, to turn things around during the show. 'I think viewers saw her as a horrible person. Now they have seen something really vulnerable about her,' she explained to *The People*.

But, describing the British public as 'evil', Katie's best mate feared that they would keep voting for the model anyway. 'The public want to see her pay, they want to see her suffer, that's the mentality of the people who hate Kate,' she said.

If the trials kept happening, she was concerned about how much more Katie could take.

On a more positive note, though, the jungle contestant's close friend insisted that, despite Katie's chat about Pete, and her tears in the jungle over the split, Alex was the man for her. 'It will have brought back memories. [But] she is completely and utterly over Pete. The minute he walked out, she stopped loving him. That's how Kate is.

'Alex makes her very happy. She has no idea that he is coming over to Australia at all; it will be a lovely surprise for her. She is very happy with him and that is the main thing.'

In fact, smitten Alex had much bigger plans than merely comforting his damsel in distress. Although he had proposed privately once before, back in September after his fight, he was now keen to make the engagement official – and planned to ask Katie to marry him in a much more public fashion as soon as she got out of the jungle.

'I'm definitely asking her to marry me,' he vowed to the *News of the World*, shortly before flying out to Brisbane. 'And I'm convinced she's going to say, "Yes."'

Indeed, when the subject of marriage came up as the campmates chatted round the blazing campfire, Katie showed very promising signs that she would like to walk down the aisle a second time – although she wasn't mentioning any names.

'I'd do it now,' she openly told former Mis-Teeq singer Sabrina Washington. 'I'm not going to wait. If it feels right, I'm going to marry straightaway. I'm thirty-one and I want to get settled down. I want to be married.'

Alex was intent on surprising Katie, who had no idea that he was heading Down Under to be with her. According to the *News of the World*, he had already picked out a £20,000 ring featuring pink diamonds. Well aware that his girlfriend had a great deal more money than him, and expensive tastes, Alex had saved every penny he could to pay for an extravagant engagement ring. 'I want the very best I can afford,' he explained to the paper. And of one thing he was certain: 'It will be a ring fit for the princess she is. One she can love and cherish. Forever.'

The tabloid also revealed that the hopeful groom-to-be thought that his romantic gesture might even be televised. 'One idea is I make the proposal in front of cameras on the show, but whatever happens, I know this is right. I've never felt this way before,' said a loved-up Alex.

'I'm convinced Katie's going to feel the same way,'

he went on. 'I know what we're like when we're together. When I'm with Katie, it's full-on 24/7.

'She ended the Pete chapter of her life in that jungle. Now it's time for her to start a new fairy tale. But this time I think it'll go the distance.'

And Katie's new Prince Charming was determined that this romance would have the perfect happy ending. After pledging to put an end to the cross-dressing that had earned him such notoriety, he reiterated his desire to have kids with the mum-of-three – and he didn't want to hang about. Alex thought three kids of their own might be ideal; with Katie's existing brood already numbering that, it was just as well that he expansively said 'the more the merrier' when it came to describing his perfect family.

The possibility that Katie might say 'no' was rejected out of hand. 'I know what I want and I'm going to get it. This love is worth fighting for. I'd do anything to make it happen. Everything that's happening right now is what I've always wanted. I've actually envisaged this for many years.'

The romantic fighter was about to get the shock of his life.

CHAPTER EIGHT

RUMBLE IN THE JUNGLE

Back in the jungle, Katie was still clinging on to her survival – just. Word of her fragile state, and worried pleas from friends and family alike, seemed to have no effect on those who were delighting in Katie's discomfort. Her sixth Bushtucker Trial was up next, and she approached it with her usual plucky attitude in the face of adversity.

Trial number six saw her covered in oil, eating fried bugs and retrieving stars from thick cobwebs housing huge spiders. The task was not as horrific as some of her previous ordeals, however, and she sailed through it, cracking jokes all the way. She told Ant and Dec that the fried cockroach tasted 'like pork scratchings' and even admitted, 'I must give it to you, that was fun.'

But her good humour hid the pain and torment she was really feeling as she let slip, 'This is so mentally torturing, I can't tell you.' And the sixth trial, while the easiest yet, ultimately proved to be the straw that broke the camel's back.

As Katie headed triumphantly back to the camp, with an impressive eleven stars out of twelve, her parting quip was, 'I'll be putting my feet up all afternoon like a princess.' At the same time, she couldn't help but betray what was really on her mind when she added, 'Love you, kids.'

For the truth was, Katie was missing her children dreadfully. The devoted mum was used to being away from her kids for short periods of time, mostly while they were with Pete, but she always spoke to them on a daily basis. After a week in the jungle, which had not only left her feeling vulnerable and persecuted, but also enforced an absolute separation from her children, she was simply desperate to be with Harvey, Junior and Princess. The pain of being apart was becoming unbearable and, as Katie trudged back to camp through the Australian rainforest, listening to the unfamiliar noise of the jungle all around her, her thoughts were never far from home.

And when Ant and Dec revealed that the public had voted her to do a seventh trial, she'd had enough.

The thought of facing a multitude of new horrors in the 'Bad Pit', as the latest trial was dubbed, tipped her over the edge. After chatting with the show's producers in immediate crisis talks in the Bush Telegraph, she came out and announced 'I'm going home' to her fellow contestants.

'Is there anything we, as a group, can do to change your mind?' asked Justin Ryan.

'No, because I would be sitting here thinking, "What are the reasons I'm staying here?"' she insisted. 'It's not even about the trial, it's about myself. I can't satisfy everyone for the rest of my life. I've got to think about me and my little chicks, my family.

'The cheque is always attractive, but it's not as if I don't earn at home. I got my husband and my children because of here and coming back was a big circle for me. I tackled it, I didn't break down and I was strong. But this is a unique place to meet someone and I have sat there, picturing things, and I've dealt with it. But I have done the hard bit that I need[ed] to do.'

As the others rallied round, asking if she was sure she was doing the right thing, she told them, 'When Pricey makes a decision, she sticks to it.'

In the Bush Telegraph, she explained that she

had done what she had come to do: put the Katie and Peter fairy tale behind her.

'There are constant reminders in here, but I've closed it, and that's all that really mattered to me,' she said.

If she hadn't won the public over with her courageous antics, she had certainly gained a few admirers in the camp. Even Kim, who had given her a hard time a few days before, had to admit, 'I like the girl. I think she's a gutsy broad.'

Staunch supporter Gino was sad to see his new pal go. 'We were all shocked that a strong woman like that would give up, just like that,' he confessed. 'So we were all a bit disappointed and all a bit shocked. But that's Katie Price!'

Only George Hamilton took the cynical view that even this move was designed to grab the most attention from the world's media. 'I think she'll get a lot more press out of it this way,' he told the others. 'I don't think it's a dumb move, it's a smart move.'

As Katie headed back to the Palazzo Versace Hotel for a long bath, a fabulous meal and a reunion with friend Michelle Heaton, she was looking forward to seeing Alex, too, but had no idea that he was already on his way, equally desperate to see her.

But the long-awaited reunion of the lovers was not to be. After Michelle revealed that Alex had sold the story of his impending proposal to a tabloid, Katie was absolutely furious.

'I don't want him near me,' she fumed to her publicist, Diana, on *What Katie Did Next*. 'He's going to do a story about our relationship anyway. Just let him do it.'

At the hotel, as the model mulled over the unhappy situation, she sought advice from her best friends – Michelle, Gary Cockerill and his husband Phil Turner – but, ultimately, she knew she had a tough choice ahead, and that she was the only one who could make it. 'I've just come out [of the jungle],' she eventually concluded. 'I need to assess the situation and I don't care what everyone's saying.'

After a good night's sleep, she headed back to the edge of the jungle to chat to Ant and Dec in her exit interview – and dropped a bombshell.

As the presenters asked about her lover's well-publicized plans to propose, she replied, 'I've done a lot of reflecting and I think it's best I'm on my own. I just don't want to be in a relationship. I hope we can remain friends, but, as of when I came out, I'm not with him.'

Her next sentence hinted at the reason behind the split.

'I know people might think it's harsh, but [...] lots of things shouldn't have happened while I was in there and they have,' she explained. 'I can't live my life by everyone else, I have to think of me and my children and I am so much happier as a person.'

Telling the hosts that she had no regrets about walking out, she reviewed her jungle experience and acknowledged that returning to the place where she and Pete had met had been an emotionally tough challenge.

'I thought I'd walk into camp and break down, but I didn't, I stayed strong. I was on the same bed, which was ironic, and I'd wake up in the morning, look over and expect to see Pete.'

The flood of memories was hard to cope with. Every time she recalled something with a smile, she'd remember in the next heartbeat that the fairy tale hadn't lasted, so every good memory was bittersweet. She could recall the happy times she and Pete had shared, but that was all gone now, never to return. Katie was proud of how she'd coped with the experience, but said, 'If I stayed any longer, it would [have got] tougher, because I'd closed it. That's one of the main reasons [I left].'

Another was, of course, her children. She revealed how much she had been missing the kids – and said that the relentless trials had also been a factor in her decision.

'With my children, I've been away a week before, but I am able to see them on Skype and I can talk to them, but I had no contact with them, which I knew [beforehand would happen], but I found it really, really hard. It made me realize I don't need to win this, it's not about that. I need to get out of here.

'Plus the trials – I am a human being and you can only take so much beating.'

She also opened her heart about her behaviour since her split with Pete and vowed to make a fresh start. In the jungle, she'd had time to think about the past few months and how she had behaved in the wake of the break-up. Mulling it over in the quiet of the rainforest, without the constant need to put a brave face on things, she had reached a sort of peace with herself at last.

Saying she had acted like 'a right fool' and a 'twit', Katie apologized to anyone she had upset – and explained that the outrageous antics were simply her way of dealing with things.

Now, though, she was truly ready to turn over a new leaf and make a fresh start. Sadly for Alex, he wasn't part of that resolution, and he found himself out in the cold as Katie looked to the future – alone.

Later, in the opulent surroundings of his hotel, a heartbroken Alex was left to deal with the news that she had dumped him on live TV. He'd been en route to Australia when Katie made her public announcement – but landing had not left him feeling like he'd returned to solid ground. It would be a while before that happened.

Meanwhile, Katie's brother Danny had just stepped off his plane and joined his sister at her hotel, where he told her, 'Alex is a good bloke.'

'It's probably a bit harsh, dumping someone on live TV,' he continued to the *What Katie Did Next* cameras. 'It's probably the top of the top one hundred things not to do when you want to break up a relationship, but hey, this is Kate. She'll do the things that aren't the norm.'

A shell-shocked Katie was trying to come to terms with her decision. After the turmoil of the jungle, she had been looking forward to getting back to normal, with both the children and Alex around her in the run-up to Christmas. Although she appeared calm, she was in fact chewed up about the split – but was nevertheless adamant that Alex had crossed a line.

'I feel very used,' she said on her TV show. 'I feel misled. What is going on? Is money important to him, or fame? As soon as I got in [the jungle], he couldn't wait to do stories. I've told him time and time again not to do any stories, to stay away from the media and for him to stick to fighting while I stick to my job. I just don't think he understands they wouldn't be interested in him if it wasn't for me.'

She also revealed that he was on his way to see her, but that she had negotiated a quick getaway with ITV bosses, so that she could head home to her family immediately, instead of sitting out her contract until 4 December as originally agreed.

'I got a text saying, "I'm on my way asap. You're the love of my life. You're worth fighting for." But now I've wangled it that I can go home early to see the children; I'm actually leaving tomorrow. I've done a lot of thinking and I'm not putting up with it.'

Nonetheless, she admitted that she was dreading spending Christmas, the first since her split with

Pete, alone. December was just around the corner and the prospect of celebrating the festive season as a single divorced woman was a lonely one. The fact that she and Pete would have to share the kids on the day was another heartache. As Katie succinctly said, 'What a shit end to the year.'

The final commitment on Katie's jungle contract was a scheduled appearance on the ITV2 sister show, *I'm a Celebrity ... Get Me Out of Here! NOW!* During the interview, Katie refused to answer questions about Alex, but managed to put a brave face on her turmoil. Laughing with presenter Caroline Flack, she revealed she had not slept alone after escaping the jungle.

'I felt fantastic this morning,' she grinned. 'I had Michelle Heaton next to me in bed and it was an eventful night. We spent the night eating and it wasn't smelling of perfume in our room this morning.'

And she said she had spoken to her kids straight-away, and that her early exit had got the support of her mum and brother Danny. 'I rang my mum as soon as I got out and I expected her to say, "What are you doing? Get back in there," but she said, "We're so proud of you and what you've done."'

Back at the hotel, the waiting press corps wanted a debrief too, so Katie explained her exit from the jungle one last time in a media conference. She also commented that, despite the horrific ordeals she had suffered, she had in fact welcomed the 'punishment'.

'I enjoyed it because I kind of like to torture myself. It was like, it's as if that is the punishment I needed,' she said. 'Not that I needed punishment, but with all what happened, it's like I really got it in there with the trials, the emotion. I felt like I was punished in there.

'So the whole experience was very weird and emotionally up and down.'

For Katie, who had made a point of not crying over her divorce, at least in public, the cathartic opportunity had been vital. As well as allowing her to vent feelings that may have been bottled up for months, the experience had also caused her to reassess her priorities, and had made her a stronger person. From here on in, she said, she was not going to try to satisfy other people. As of now, it was her and her kids who were coming first. She was taking control, and refused to allow herself to be 'pulled here, there and everywhere', even in the pursuit of success. As she reasoned, 'Take everything away, all what's left would be me and my kids, my family and friends. And that is worth more to me than big houses, cars, money, because you've always got that unit. I found out it was important before, but it's made me realize that it is so much more important to me than anything.'

Her assessment of life was a fruitful and positive one. But having vowed to put relationships before business, Katie was struck by the sudden hole in her life that marked Alex's absence. While she put a brave face on the split, even tweeting, 'I feeeel sooo goood today' shortly after the announcement that she was single, she was actually finding the reality of living without her other half painful.

So much so that, back in her hotel room, she decided to grant Alex some time to talk, to explain her decision and express her anger at his betrayal. The former couple planned crisis talks about their relationship and Alex was asked to come over to Katie's suite for the crucial conversation. Katie felt she owed Alex an explanation at the very least, while he was desperate to see her in order to plead his case and give his side of the story.

Conscious of her vulnerable emotional state, however, Katie made sure she was surrounded by her closest circle first. 'I'm hoping to see Alex to have a chat while my brother and Diana are here, just to go through things in his head, the reason why I'm not with him,' she explained on *What Katie Did Next*.

Alex had only one shot at persuading her to change her mind, as Katie continued, 'Once I leave here, I'm not going to go back and meet with him in England to go through it. I want to do it now. It's so sad, such a shame. I'm still shocked that it's happened. I think I'm emotionally drained [after] the past two weeks.'

Concerned friend Michelle was on standby as Katie and Alex locked themselves into an upstairs room in the model's spacious suite. 'I think Alex is a really great guy,' admitted her pal. 'I'm just not sure he's the right guy for Kate.'

After two hours, when there was no word from Katie, and the group was still waiting to go out for dinner, Michelle was beginning to get worried. She decided to send her friend a text to see if she was all right, although she joked that she didn't rate her chances against professional fighter Alex if she had to come between the two.

Pondering the closed door of the room in which the couple talked, Gary weighed up the odds of what was happening. Were the pair arguing, or kissing and making up? Having spent time talking with Katie about her feelings, he revealed that she had 'got it into her head' that Alex wasn't right for her and that she shouldn't be his girlfriend. Was this a fight Alex could win? The odds seemed stacked against him.

In Britain, worried mum Carol Reid was desperate to get hold of her heartbroken son. Unhappy that he had been dumped on live TV, she blasted Katie's 'cruel' treatment of him.

'It seemed very cruel the way she spoke about Alex. He really loved her and gave up a lot for her and this is how he gets treated,' she fretted in the *Mirror*. 'All I know is that he is in Australia and his phone is off. He must be upset. I am worried for him.'

Three hours after going into the bedroom, Katie and Alex emerged – together. The romance was back on, Alex was almost forgiven, but he was still on probation in Katie's eyes. 'It's fine if he wants to be with me for me, but he needs to prove it,' said a feisty Kate.

Her muscle-bound boyfriend was mortified that he had upset the love of his life, and was deeply worried that he was not going to be able to make it up to her. 'I've got a good connection with this woman. I only have honourable intentions,' he vowed on-screen on *What Katie Did Next*. And he was quick to dismiss the idea that he was only with Katie because of her high profile. 'I hate this celebrity shit. I don't care about fame. I go to sleep thinking about her and I wake up thinking about her.'

For Katie's part, it turned out that, despite what she viewed as Alex's betrayal, her feelings for him were too intense to be ignored. 'I looked at him and I thought, "I'm so into you. I want to be with you."' It was as simple as that.

The method Katie had chosen to end the relationship did not escape mention from the jilted Alex, though. He expressed his disbelief at the way she had ended it. 'To be dumped, on national TV, I couldn't believe it. I love this woman one hundred per cent.'

But in her defence, Katie said, 'I was so pissed off, so angry.'

At the end of the day, the truth of her feelings for Alex was impossible to deny. Despite the tabloid story, despite Katie's fear that things might not work out, she had to give it one last try. Not to do so would be to give in, to shy away from love – and if there is one thing Katie Price is not, it's a coward. Head high, and with her heart back in Alex's safe keeping, she was risking everything for her man.

With a slightly brittle tone that betrayed her vulnerability, she closed the subject as she said, 'Let's hope [Alex] doesn't end up breaking my heart. If things work out, it will be fabulous. If not, it will just be me, my kids and my horses – and we'll be fine.'

While Katie was prepared to give her man a second chance, she wasn't letting him off the hook straightaway. And she wasn't about to retract her rejection in public, either.

In her first magazine interview after leaving the jungle, she told *Hello!*: 'Strangely enough, I feel more hurt from this split than I did with Pete, because I had known for some time from seeing a marriage counsellor that it probably wouldn't have lasted. Lots of things had happened, whereas with Alex, it seem[ed] a fresh start.'

She confirmed that the split had been caused by Alex selling a story about their relationship to a Sunday newspaper, but hinted that the liaison wasn't completely over when she was asked about what the future now held for the couple.

'It's very hard to say what will transpire between us because at the moment I'm absolutely livid about the whole situation. He has been very naive and people are taking advantage of him. If things get sorted out, then fabulous. If not, I'll be on my own.'

And she admitted, 'I was really falling for the guy and I can't just switch off feelings. I'm not entirely ruling out anything between us.'

In an expression of the new self-awareness she had achieved in the jungle, she also said that she understood why people had voted for her to complete every trial on *I'm a Celebrity ... Get Me Out of Here!* 'While I was in the jungle, I could see why people blew up and were furious,' she commented. Yet with characteristic bluntness, she defiantly continued, 'But I can't regret what I've done in the past because it reflected how I felt and I thought it was right at the time.'

Although she now knew that she wanted to be with Alex, Katie was still letting him sweat a little. In the days after the crisis talks, she continued to keep their reunion quiet and Alex was forced to play the part of a spurned lover in the face of the world's press. The couple avoided each other at the Versace Hotel for the five days before Katie flew back to

England, alone. Asked about the split, Alex had clearly learned his lesson and was not about to blab to the papers, offering only, 'I've had better weeks.'

Later, Katie would blame her close-knit circle for the break-up. 'I was poisoned and he was poisoned by people around us,' she told DJ Chris Moyles on his Radio 1 breakfast show. 'We met up in Australia and made up and we've been together ever since.'

She would also go on to admit – despite what she'd said in her *Hello!* interview about no regrets – that she did regret her hasty decision to finish with Alex. 'That is a regret,' she told *OK!* in February. 'Even when I said on *I'm a Celebrity* that we were over, I wanted to be with him.

'It won't happen again. All Alex wants is to be good at what he does, have a family and settle down.'

For his part, Alex was happy to take the blame and was quick to confess that his naivety may have been a factor. 'It was basically a big misunderstanding,' he told *Star* magazine, giving his version of events. 'There were a lot of poisonous things said on both sides. And I was naive to trust certain people.'

He also revealed his true feelings over the split, and said that despite the very public dumping, he always knew in his heart that it wasn't final. 'It was horrible [at the time],' he admitted, 'but I never thought that was the end. There was just a lot of overreaction on both sides. And we got back together later, but kept it quiet. We just had to clear the air.'

As he landed at Heathrow the day after Kate, unbeknown to the hordes of paparazzi waiting to snap the 'broken-hearted' beau, Alex was actually looking forward to one of Katie's famous Sunday roasts – and he was determined to make up for his mistakes in any way he could. His naivety had nearly cost him the love of his life. From here on in, Alex Reid was determined to play it safe, to play by the rules – and to play to win the heart of Katie Price, once and for all.

CHAPTER NINE

CHRISTMAS TEARS

KATIE'S OWN PLANE touched down at Heathrow on Saturday 28 November and she put her troubled relationship firmly to the back of her mind. She had three important reasons to celebrate life and they were waiting to be reunited with their mum.

The emotional reunion at her Surrey home had been delayed longer than she'd expected, however, as she'd had trouble finding a flight home immediately. Now, she couldn't wait to hug Harvey, Junior and Princess.

Bursting through the door, she kissed and hugged her children as she told them, 'I've missed you so much.'

With December approaching, Katie's thoughts were naturally turning to Christmas, one of her favourite times of year, and she was looking forward to treating the kids. 'Xmas spirit started,' she posted on Twitter, three days after her return, 'took kids to harrods to see santa they loved it … advent calender starts an put xmas trees up today woooo.'

But her lovely surprise backfired – and sparked a new row with Pete – when a Sunday newspaper reported that her ex had in fact arranged a two-hour visit to the top London store for the following day. 'It was going to be a really special day,' a Harrods source told the *News of the World*, 'but in walked Jordan with the kids and she demanded the same thing we were going to do for Peter.'

The couple's first Christmas apart was bound to cause more friction between them. After enjoying family celebrations together for six years, first with Harvey and later with their own two, the heartache of sharing the kids over the festive season was beginning to hit home. The issue was complicated by the serious illness of Pete's father, Savva, in Australia. His worried son was planning to dash home straight after Christmas to see his dad, and he wanted to take the children to see their granddad, possibly for the last time.

'I want to be with my kids at Christmas, but I honestly don't know at this point what's happening, which is madness,' Peter told *OK!* magazine in mid

December. 'I really don't want to think about not seeing them on Christmas Day. I'm still going to have my time to give them presents whatever.

'There's a chance I may well be in Australia. If I am and the kids are with me, I'll do something with my family. But if I'm on my own, I know where to party with my mates and brothers.'

Katie, however, was not willing to be separated from the children for more than a week so soon after her own trip to Australia. She had found the time without them too painful to repeat and decided to veto his plans. But she did offer a compromise over the festive period, generously allowing him to have Junior and Princess on Christmas Day. She would spend the day with Harvey and the rest of her family, and would celebrate with the younger children on Boxing Day instead.

The warring couple, who had publicly fought for seven months, declared a truce over Christmas for the sake of the children. Back on speaking terms with her ex, and back on track with Alex, Katie was still geared up for an emotional time and knew it would bring back memories.

'Christmas is going to be hurtful,' she admitted to *OK!*, but vowed to turn to her mum, brother Danny and sister Sophie for support. 'The whole family is deciding what we're doing for Christmas this year, which is really exciting.'

In a rare period of privacy, the media target had somehow managed to keep Alex's reappearance in her life a secret. Respecting her wishes, the sheepish fighter was lying low and, while they were in constant touch on the phone, they saw little of each other and were especially careful not to be seen in public together.

Three weeks on, the anger had gone and Katie was madly in love again. In a typically showy gesture, she chose to announce that she and Alex were once again an item by taking him along to the most high-profile show on television – *The X Factor* final. The couple were invited by friend Simon Cowell as his surprise guests.

Though the building was heaving with journalists, the couple still went to extraordinary lengths to avoid being pictured together outside the Fountain Studios in London. First Alex hid in a burger restaurant while Katie made her grand entrance, then he nipped in a side door and joined her in the hospitality area. Once inside, however, the loved-up model was happy to spill the beans.

Left: The family out shopping in Brighton in September 2009. Katie was heard telling photographers that she would marry Alex.

Below: This is serious: Katie and Alex gaze into each other's eyes at the Horse of the Year Show in October 2009.

Above: Katie launches her book *Standing Out* with a little help from her friends (from left to right: Alex Reid, Andrew Gould, Daniel Price and Phil Turner).

Right: Alex – as his cross-dressing alter ego Roxanne – and Katie at the Bloodlust Ball in London.

Facing page: Katie at a book signing.

Left: She's back: Katie heads to the jungle for her second stint on *I'm a Celebrity*.

Below: Gutted: Alex at Brisbane Airport after Katie dumped him live on TV. He had reportedly flown out to propose to her.

Left: Katie returns to the UK alone following the split.

Above: 'I want to turn these boos into cheers': Alex chats to host Davina McCall prior to entering the *Celebrity Big Brother* house in January 2010.

Left: He's a winner: Alex triumphs on the show with 65.9% of the vote. Here he is with his fellow housemates at the final, including Katie's ex Dane Bowers (right).

While Alex is away …
Katie dazzles at the
National Television
Awards during Alex's
CBB stint.

Decisions, decisions: Katie and Alex shop for wedding rings in America.

Above: The wedding salon at the Wynn Hotel in Vegas where Katie and Alex tied the knot.

Left: Loving mum: Katie spends some time with her daughter the day before leaving for Las Vegas.

Katie shows off her sparkler as the couple seal their marriage with a kiss.

'We haven't announced we are back together. We're seeing how it goes,' she admitted to the *Mirror*. 'I don't care what anyone thinks – it's up to me who I go out with.'

Katie also flashed a large diamond ring on her left hand, teasing the press with, 'I always wear this ring on my engagement finger – it doesn't mean anything really.'

During the night, she took Alex to Simon's dressing room to introduce him: a sure sign that her lover had finally been forgiven for his indiscretion.

In the weeks running up to the public reunion, Alex had been building bridges, as well as negotiating a TV career of his own. The fame and notoriety he had gained since he began dating Katie had led to a lucrative offer to star in *Celebrity Big Brother*. While he had been warned off making money from selling their love secrets, he felt the opportunity – and the cheque, reported to be £150,000 – was too good to miss.

Katie was initially wary. She was still smarting from the fact that he had made money by talking about her to the papers and she hated the idea of anyone achieving fame and fortune on her coat-tails. After long discussions about Alex's future, however, she accepted that he wanted to do this for himself, so that the public could see him as his own man, not just Jordan's latest boyfriend.

Shrewd as ever, she also realized that the public had only ever read negative stories about the man she loved. A stint in the *Big Brother* house would show the world what she already knew – that Alex Reid was a decent, thoughtful and truly likeable guy. She finally agreed that he could go into the house, but not before she had laid down a few ground rules. Discussions about her divorce, her fights with Pete and their sex life were completely off-limits and, in order to stay in control, she warned him not to drink too much and start blabbing about their relationship. In the weeks running up to the show, she also gave him tips on how to behave and how to present himself to the media.

'I thought it had its pros and cons,' she explained later to *OK!* magazine. 'I did feel like people would see what he's really like, but a show like that can be edited to make him look bad, so I was worried about that.

'But then we decided it was a good idea that Alex went in and I said to him, "Show them what you're about, don't talk about me all the time." Not because

I was being controlling, but because I wanted people to see him in his own right.'

'We hoped that maybe they would get to see I'm a nice guy,' added Alex.

Channel 4 executives were delighted when Alex accepted the offer, but – in typical *Big Brother* style – they had a surprise up their sleeve for the fledgling celebrity. Katie's ex Dane Bowers, the man she had called the love of her life in her autobiography, would also be entering the notorious house.

Katie had been devastated by the end of their eighteen-month relationship, back when she was twenty-one, and had even admitted to taking an overdose over the boy-band star. Now the man she had once loved would go head to head with her current love for four weeks, under the unforgiving gaze of the British public.

Worried about how that might work, Katie decided it would be a good idea to introduce the men before they met in the *Big Brother* house. A New Year's Eve party at her house seemed the perfect opportunity.

In the meantime, she had Christmas Day to worry about. On 24 December, she tweeted, 'I hate being without princess an junior at christmas :(but can't wait to get them back tom night as pete goes to oz for 2 weeks.'

On Christmas morning, as she sat watching Harvey opening his presents without his little brother and sister, she held back tears. Her first Christmas since her marriage broke down was proving incredibly painful, as she had predicted. The absence of her two youngest children added to the heartache and highlighted the fracturing of the family that the split had brought about.

Cuddling her seven-year-old son, surrounded by discarded wrapping paper, brand-new toys and piles of unopened gifts, she reflected that her declaration in the days running up to Christmas had proved all too accurate. As she had wrapped presents by herself some hours earlier, she had announced to her reality-show cameras, 'In thirty-one years, this is the worst Christmas I have ever had.' It most definitely was.

As well as messing up her festive celebrations, the uncertainty with the children had meant that she and Alex had been forced to shelve another secret plan – to get hitched before he entered the *Big Brother* house. After they finally tied the knot in February, Katie told Chris Moyles, 'We were going to do it at Christmas, but we didn't have time because of the kids' situation and Pete going to Australia. We always knew we were going to do it straightaway.'

The anxious mum was delighted to get her youngest children back in the early evening of 25 December, but the reunion was marred by a small detail, which was to break the tentative truce between the divorcees and cause another, very public, row. While staying with her dad, Princess Tiaamii had been given a haircut by Peter's hairdresser brother Michael.

'Can't believe that when I got kids back princess comes back with her hair all cut short soo out of order,' Katie posted on Twitter at 2 a.m. on Boxing Day morning. She followed it with the loaded suggestion that the hair had been cut to prove a point. 'Pete brother has cut princesses hair off can't put it in a pony tail why would they do that to prove what point.'

Pete was amazed by the reaction to his daughter's hair and fired back at his ex-wife over the issue of her using hair straighteners on the little girl. 'Kate wrote something on Twitter over Christmas about it being out of order that my brother Mike cut Princess's hair and that we did it to prove a point,' he told *new!* magazine later. 'The truth of the matter is I have noticed lately that someone has been straightening Princess's hair with straightening irons and the ends were getting damaged. Why a girl of two needs straight hair is beyond me, but obviously it's something Kate has decided to do and I can't stop her.

'Mike is a professional hairdresser and he literally took the ends off my daughter's hair to tidy it up. It really wasn't a big deal.'

On Boxing Day, with hostilities reopened, a saddened Pete left the country without the children for two weeks. While he was away, the Kat was certainly going to play, with a party that was set to cause more gossip in the papers and leave her under attack once again.

As a new year dawned, Kate, Alex and Dane found themselves embroiled in a fresh controversy.

CHAPTER TEN

BOOZE, BRAWLS AND *BB* BOOS

ALTHOUGH IT HAD brought her together with Alex, 2009 was a year that Katie was keen to forget. It had seen her family split in two and she had endured a painful divorce, being pilloried in the press and a torturous time in the jungle.

'I've worked out the number nine was unlucky for me,' she said portentously on *GMTV*. 'Dwight's shirt was number nine, I got married in September and the year 09 was a bad omen.'

As 2010 loomed, Katie Price was determined to put her troubles behind her and start again. What better way to mark the arrival of a new chapter in her life than to surround herself with family and friends – and party!

Katie sent out invitations for a massive NYE fancy-dress do, instructing guests that the theme was 'Enchanted, Magical, Disney or Wow Factor' and making it quite clear that no costume meant no entry. She hired a DJ, a huge karaoke machine and a team of nannies to look after the twenty children who would be there.

She and Alex spent hours browsing the shelves of Angels, the theatrical costumiers and fancy-dress suppliers, for the perfect outfit in which to bowl over their guests … but an excited Katie simply failed to narrow it down. In the end, she planned to wow the party with no less than three fancy-dress outfits – a pumpkin suit, dog-slayer Cruella DeVille and finally Minnie Mouse. She also chose Disney costumes for her three children, including Buzz Lightyear for Junior and, appropriately, a princess outfit for Princess Tiiaami. Alex, meanwhile, found himself a Roman gladiator suit, which – to his girlfriend's delight – showcased his bulging muscles.

On the night, Katie was on top form. The large living room in her Surrey mansion was adorned with lavish Christmas decorations and heaving with bodies. Dane Bowers duly arrived in a Zorro outfit and Alex, turning up in his revealing toga, was rewarded with a passionate kiss from his lady. Other guests included best pals Michelle Heaton, Gary Cockerill and Phil Turner, as well as celebrities such as Simon Webbe and Lee Ryan, who belted out a version of their song 'All Rise' on the karaoke machine.

Katie herself sang 'The Final Countdown' shortly before midnight, before shouting, 'I hate 2009. Hate, hate, hate it.' Then she yelled, 'Happy New Year!' and kissed the man who would make 2010 a special one for her.

Alex was in his element, surrounded by colourful characters in outrageous outfits and standing beside the love of his life. He was about to embark on a new career as a TV star in his own right and he couldn't have been happier. The loved-up couple were looking forward to a new start.

The bubble burst two days later – when rumours of a fight between Alex and Dane were leaked to the papers. Reports that the duo had come to blows after Katie's ex blasted her for letting the children stay up too late made headlines, and Dane appeared to be sporting a cut above his eye and bruises on his arm and shoulders.

Both Dane and Alex hotly denied the reports. Twenty-four hours later, just minutes before Alex entered the *Big Brother* house, *BB* host Davina McCall directly asked the cage fighter if he had been involved in a brawl at the house.

'Categorically no,' said Alex, who had been booed by the crowd on his way in. 'I didn't even know there was a fight until after. This is why I am here: to change the boos into cheers.'

Dane's injuries were obvious as he walked up the steps to the house. In a later interview, he confessed a scuffle had taken place, but not with his new housemate.

'I'm not sure what the eye [injury] was,' he told *new!* magazine. 'I think the eye was when I fell down the stairs by Jordan's bathroom at the New Year's Eve party. The shoulder one was a scrape I had on the floor. There was a little altercation with a couple of people that night.'

More worryingly for Katie, Peter Andre was said to be furious about the party and the fact that pictures of his tired children had emerged on a social networking site. With the custody battle ongoing, the concerned mum could not afford to hand him any more ammunition. But she refuted any suggestion that the party had called her mothering skills into question.

'The reason I had a New Year's Eve party is because a lot of my friends have children that are Princess, Harvey and Junior's age,' she told Kate

Garraway on *GMTV*. 'And there were about twenty children there. It's New Year's Eve and lots of kids are up. We have a nurse who works for [a children's hospital] and works for me a few hours a week, and she also deals with kids that are abused and reports them to social services. If I was such a bad mum, she wouldn't have been with me for three years and she would have reported me.'

As the old adage goes, no publicity is bad publicity, and the reports of the NYE party did serve to up the interest in the seventh and final series of *Celebrity Big Brother*. Regular viewers were joined by gossip fans as the first eleven celebs to enter the house were unveiled on Sunday 3 January.

The baying crowd outside the house shouted 'fight, fight, fight' as Dane, who had been warned away from conflict by worried producers, denied any friction between him and Alex.

'I'm sorry to disappoint you, but we actually get on,' he told Davina McCall. 'He's a cool guy and we actually get on OK.'

But as he entered the house, shortly after Alex, the country waited with bated breath to see how they would greet each other. Dane just grinned at his 'love rival' and joked, 'Round two?' before hugging him and slapping him on the back, saying, 'How you doing, buddy?' Then he dismissed questions from housemate Nicola T about his black eye, replying, 'It's a boo-boo from a couple of days ago. I've got make-up on it.'

The two men were joined in the *Celebrity Big Brother* house by an eclectic bunch of personalities. Hollywood celebs Vinnie Jones, Stephanie Beacham and Stephen Baldwin made the line-up, along with Page Three girl Nicola T, former madam Heidi Fleiss, R&B singers Sisqó and Jonas Altberg, Brit rapper Lady Sovereign and recent girlfriend of Rolling Stone Ronnie Wood, Ekaterina Ivanova.

The design of the new house was based on Dante's *Inferno*, with a red-and-black entrance decorated with flames. Inside, a red carpet covered the living-room floor and plush red sofas were scattered with cushions bearing pictures of horned skeletons and animal skulls. The kitchen was based on an autopsy laboratory and the entrance to the Diary Room resembled the mouth of an inferno, with flames licking up the walls. The bathroom was more like heaven – with a cream chaise longue, a dressing table and a free-standing Victorian-style bath.

The garden contained a snug, complete with two couches and a fireplace, as well as the Tree of

Temptation, which was designed to whisper to the housemates when they were alone in the garden.

Alex entered the house as an outsider, with odds of 14–1. He was apparently already disliked by the show's fans, hence the booing and heckling as he climbed the famous stairs to the door. Even his mum wasn't optimistic about his chances.

'He won't stay in until the end,' said Carol to the *Sunday Mirror*. 'We just hope he stays in long enough for people to see the real him. As long as he doesn't say anything too stupid, he should be OK. He can't fight for ever. He needs a career.'

Alex was initially nervous as he walked through the hallowed doors, but Big Brother helped the housemates break the ice by asking them to pile into a Mini on the lawn, meaning they got up close and personal within hours of meeting each other.

The day after Alex entered the house, Katie went to Twitter to report a new twist in the tale about which she had heard rumours – and to reveal that she wasn't the only woman whom Alex and Dane had shared.

'Gossip: heard a model called vicky thomas who is an ex of danes an alexes is going in house bring it on bb how funny love it xx' she tweeted on 4 January.

But the rumours turned out to be false and the only other person to enter the house, on day six, was millionaire divorcee Ivana Trump.

Viewers expecting Alex to become Roxanne in the house were sorely disappointed when he revealed that he had left his more feminine items of clothing behind. Stephen Baldwin asked him what he had packed for his stay and Alex, who was keen to distance himself from the cross-dressing tag, replied, 'All Arthur, no Martha!'

And he rubbished claims that the show's bosses had offered him a huge amount of money to wear women's clothes. 'They wrote that I'd been offered an extra £100,000 to wear a dress,' he told Stephen. 'I'd wear a dress for a hundred grand!'

Even *Dynasty* legend Stephanie Beacham seemed to be somewhat crestfallen to find herself sharing house space with the real Alex Reid, rather than his alter ego, complaining that she had expected a 'cross-dressing bad boy'.

'I dress up for fun,' he explained to Nicola T. 'They've just blown it way out of proportion. If it's going to get me a hot woman, which it did, I'll dress up whatever.'

On another occasion, a curious Vinnie dragged

Alex into yet another discussion about his cross-dressing. In a cringe-making interrogation, the former footballer would not let the subject drop.

'Why did you tell the papers that?' he asked.

'I went out on a school night out. I'm ex-army, we dress up for a laugh. I was in the army for three or four years and it's a laugh, so what?' replied Alex. 'They got hold of it and made a big thing.'

'So it was a night out, fancy dress, you don't think, "I'm gonna sit at home in my dress tonight"?' persisted Vinnie.

'I don't go down the supermarket.'

Unwilling to relinquish the subject, Vinnie then asked him directly if he ever sat at home in a dress. A clearly embarrassed Alex laughed, 'I have done … not on my own. I've done it for a laugh to see what it's all about, with a "friend" of mine. It's no big deal. Some people like to wear nappies …'

'But some people keep that to themselves and don't let the newspapers know about it,' concluded Vinnie.

In fact, it was Dane who found himself dressing in women's clothing, when he and Alex were set a particularly hilarious task. Picked to perform a duet together, Alex dressed as Jason Donovan and Dane as Kylie Minogue. While Katie watched with her friends at home, doubled over with fits of laughter, the unlikely duo warbled their way through 'Especially For You' – to the delight of *CBB* fans.

While they weren't getting to meet Roxanne, viewers were certainly getting a pound or two of flesh. The muscle-bound fighter seemed to be stripping off at the drop of a hat, and his naked antics were amusing everyone – even his mum.

'He gets his exhibitionism from his dad,' she told the *Sunday Mirror*. 'But I don't squirm when I see him taking his clothes off on telly because that's just him. If he was sitting here right now, he'd be in his pants. He always has his clothes off.

'But he's just very comfortable with his body. He'll get up in the morning, come downstairs and put the kettle on, semi-naked.' And with two exhibitionists in the family, she joked, 'Sunday lunch can be interesting.'

On day five, Alex took part in a 'hunk off' against four of the other lads. They each had to choose a Borat-style mankini and parade down a catwalk while the ladies looked on and gave them scores out of ten, as well as doing a strength test, which involved opening a jar of pickles, and taking part in a talent show.

Vinnie Jones ruled himself out of the challenge by bagging the job of task coordinator, but he couldn't resist the temptation to take the mickey out of Alex.

When Alex, dressed in a pink mankini, came fourth out of five, Vinnie told the others that Alex wasn't happy with the result. And when Alex proclaimed he 'had to win something', the Hollywood hardman teased, 'What are the odds in [your next] fight? My money's on the other bloke.'

Watching Alex performing a series of press-ups, Vinnie remarked, 'If he was made of chocolate, he'd eat himself, wouldn't he?'

More annoyingly for Alex, Dane came second in the swimwear section, despite refusing to wear a mankini and being issued vest and shorts instead.

Task producer Daniel Nettleton explained that the *Big Brother* team had come up with the task idea because of Alex's tendency to strip. 'We've seen Alex with no clothes on – so we're going to see the rest of them with no clothes on,' he commented.

Away from the tasks, with little to do but chat, Alex found himself breaking Katie's number-one rule – and talking about their relationship. After just one day, mischievous Vinnie Jones sparked a conversation about the glamour girl by asking Dane when he had dated her. After the singer told him it was ten years ago, Vinnie replied, 'Oh, pre-Peter. I like Peter.'

'I'm cool with him,' Alex chipped in, although he had to admit that he had never met him.

Later, the loved-up contestant couldn't resist telling his housemates that the couple had slept together on their first night. He confided in them about meeting Katie in July and said it was 'straight back to her house the first night'. Then he added, 'A good night, though!'

Dane laughed, but Vinnie warned him that Katie would be angry that he had revealed a bedroom secret on national TV.

Clearly not too miffed, though, his girlfriend posted her support on Twitter, writing, 'Absence makes the heart grow fonder! our relationship goes beyond big brother ill be waiting with open arms ;)'

Cut off from the outside world, however, Alex began to doubt whether she would still be waiting for him when he left.

'You have a lot of time to think in there,' he admitted later to *new!* magazine. 'I was thinking, "Will she still want me when I come out?" It's silly, but a normal reaction. I knew deep down she would and the proof is in the pudding.'

While Alex attempted to stop himself talking about his partner, with limited success, Katie had no control over the mouth of ex-lover Dane. In a late-night chat with grand inquisitor Vinnie, Dane claimed he had split with the model over her naked photo shoots. He also talked about Katie's claims that he was obsessed with Victoria Beckham, with whom he was making a record at the time, and revealed that he had given her an ultimatum before they parted.

'It was lots of little things, really [behind our break-up],' he confided. 'If you hear her side of things, it was because of Victoria [Beckham], I was working too hard with Victoria.

'At the time, I was quite jealous. [Katie had] stopped doing all the nudie shoots, the really naughty things. Then she did one just to spite me, and I said, "If you do it, I'll leave you," and she did it.'

He also claimed he knew Katie better than Alex, who had 'only been with her six months', and bragged about his and Katie's notorious sex tape, saying it had helped her career and 'set her up' because his band, Another Level, were at the peak of their success at the time it came out.

Watching at home, Katie was furious with Dane for talking about her while Alex was in bed asleep. 'He talked about me a lot behind Alex's back,' she fumed, after the show was finished, to *OK!* magazine. 'He doesn't know me better than Alex. When I went out with Dane, I was nineteen. I hadn't even had Harvey. I'm thirty-one now, with three kids. I'm a different person. Alex knows me a hundred times better.'

But with Alex shut up in the *CBB* house for the foreseeable future, Katie had no way of reassuring her lover. All she could do was watch him, like the rest of the nation, as he continued on his *Big Brother* journey. Watch, and wait, and hope.

CHAPTER ELEVEN

ZERO TO HERO

NSIDE THE *Big Brother* house, the talk often turned to Katie, but outside, much of the buzz was about Alex himself. His playful antics and calm, friendly nature were beginning to win over the public – and his chances of winning began to improve with each show.

One incident, which had Katie and her pals in stitches, along with the rest of the country, was the now notorious 'spray tan episode'. The housemates had worked together to convince Ivana Trump that she had won an award and, as a reward for passing the task, they received a bag of goodies, which included a can of fake tan.

Body-conscious Alex was, inevitably, the first to strip off to be sprayed – and his fellow contestants were only too happy to help. After Jonas had covered his back, Page Three girl Nicola T set about spraying his more intimate parts for an all-over tan.

As his housemates laughed, Nicola bent down to colour his buttocks – and in between – before moving to his front, as Alex protected his modesty with a tiny towel. Vinnie stood on the sidelines, telling her to spray more on the face.

The resulting orange hue had the papers comparing him to an Oompa Loompa from *Charlie and the Chocolate Factory*, but it did Alex no harm in the popularity stakes. It was also his girlfriend's all-time favourite moment from the show.

'That is so, so nuts,' Katie said on *Big Brother's Big Mouth*. 'The pair of us, imagine what we're like together. That is brilliant, that is so Alex. He's always got his kit off, so that's not a surprise either.'

Other moments which stuck in the memory included Alex using his martial arts skills to decapitate a snowman with one kick, on the orders of *Big Brother*; getting Nicola to squeeze the spots on his back as he sat in the bath; and streaking through the house and garden, along with Basshunter aka Jonas, wearing only a blonde wig. And who could forget the night-time prank from Vinnie, who crept up to Alex's bed in the dark and tickled his toes, giving Alex the fright of his life?

One of the more touching moments saw Alex

talking religion with house zealot Stephen Baldwin, who took his hand for a prayer session as Alex asked forgiveness for his sins. He repeated Stephen's prayer and finished with 'I am willing to believe'.

As well as voicing his love for Katie, Alex demonstrated his utter admiration for her achievements when he explained why she was famous to Stephen. 'It's unreal. She's a phenomena in this country. You go to some of her book signings and there's like eight hundred, nine hundred people waiting for her. It's absolutely crazy.

'She's had a pop career. She was trying to do a bit of acting. She just went up for *Sex and the City 2*, but she's not focused on it and it's not really what her heart is in. I think she could be quite a good actress if she had the right part.'

Away from the *Big Brother* house, at their home in Aldershot, Bob and Carol Reid were watching their son's exploits with amused pride. Mum Carol, who calls the thirty-four-year-old hunk 'my baby', said to the *Sunday Mirror* that she believed he had agreed to take part in the TV show to even out his relationship with the love of his life. 'My son just wants to make his own way. He doesn't want to be a kept man. He wants to be Katie's equal in some sort of way.'

She also thought he was driven to try to banish the tabloid caricature that had somehow been built up in his image. 'He's just trying to let people see what he's really like, not the villain the public seems to think,' she said in an exclusive interview.

On the subject of her son in love, a pleased Carol was absolutely firm about the genuine nature of the relationship, revealing, 'This is the first time he's properly been in love.

'He said to me, right at the start [of his and Katie's relationship], "We just connected, Mum." Katie is The One, I have no doubt.'

Describing the model as 'his intellectual equal', Carol said she wasn't intimidated by her iconic future daughter-in-law, treating her just like she would any other girlfriend. Nevertheless, she expressed some reservations about her son's exposure to Katie's extraordinary lifestyle, with Alex finding himself cast in the full glare of the media spotlight and the subject of a million paparazzi camera flashes. Given the Australian 'proposal' debacle, it felt a little like the stable door being shut after the horse had bolted when she commented that Alex was 'naive' and 'could easily be manipulated'.

'I don't know if he's got the savvy to cope,' admitted

his concerned mum. 'He's going to have to wise up or he'll drown in Katie's world.'

With Alex currently playing to an audience of millions on national TV, his ability to handle a proper media profile was going to be put to the test before too long. But in a new twist to the rumours that Alex was only with Katie for fame, his mum's opinion was that celebrity actually 'stressed him out'.

'He wasn't prepared for that [being famous]. He just fell in love. All the other stuff – the big circus – came along afterwards,' explained Alex's number-one fan. 'But there are pros and cons to every relationship. The big pro is that they are, I think, very much in love. As far as Alex is concerned, this is the real thing.'

Certainly Katie was keen to give the impression that she, too, was genuinely in love – despite pal Michelle Heaton's slip-up on spin-off show *Big Brother's Big Mouth*, when she claimed the model 'could do better'.

Having travelled with Michelle to the studio, Katie clearly had words with her friend in the commercial break and the Liberty X singer came back on to say, 'Jordan has asked me to say that she loves Alex to bits. She is supporting him completely and they are totally an item.'

A few days later, two days before the *CBB* final, Katie tweeted in full caps to express her pride and enthusiasm: 'AMAZING AMAZING AMAZING MY BOY HAS DONE AMAZING.'

Alex's simple good-natured personality was also winning over his housemates – and he was fast becoming the most popular figure in the house. Nicola T was bowled over by his thoughtfulness, gushing to the others, 'He is one of the nicest guys I have ever met in my life. So kind, so friendly, dozy. He is such a decent guy – such a good soul. He's literally a labrador.'

On her eviction, Donald Trump's ex-wife, who has a penchant for younger men, admitted she quite fancied the British beefcake. 'Alex is hot,' she told Davina McCall. 'He's got a great body. He's a nice guy. I exercise and he gave me motivation.'

In the Diary Room, Dane revealed how well he was getting on with Alex, and how they had got over any jealousies that might have arisen. 'At first, we might have been more on our guard because of what the public perception is, but he's got more of that to deal with than me,' he said. 'He's in a really high-profile relationship. But he makes it easy as well because he's cool about it, I'm cool about it. We know what it is and it doesn't bother us.'

He did admit to Nicola that he found talking about his ex 'awkward', but Alex wasn't to blame for that. 'I find it hard talking about Kate in front of Alex,' Dane confessed, explaining, 'It's weird we have both been with the same girl.'

Even Vinnie Jones, who nicknamed Alex 'Rocky' and seemed to delight in taking the mickey out of his muscular rival, was growing to like him. 'I really feel for the fellow because he got the biggest boos going in and hopefully he will get the biggest cheers going out.'

As Alex's popularity soared, both in and out of the house, Vinnie's 'house dad' act was beginning to be seen as bossiness, even borderline bullying, and the former footballer was slowly slipping from his long-held top spot in the betting. In the race to win the *CBB* crown, Alex's odds were being constantly slashed and, ironically, his biggest rival turned out to be Dane Bowers.

On 26 January, three days before the final, the Another Level star was the even-money favourite, having started out on odds of 16–1. Two days later, with just 24 hours to go, Alex had leapfrogged Dane and slashed his original 14–1 odds to 6–5 on to win.

The beefy star had stolen the nation's heart with his affable grin, his patience and his generosity in the house. If the lurid tabloid stories about the cage fighter had led the public to expect a violent, aggressive bully, nothing could have been further from the truth. In his four weeks in the house, Alex had never shown any sign of losing his temper, even when under fire from Vinnie, and had treated his fellow housemates with consideration and respect throughout.

As the five finalists – Alex, Dane, Stephanie, Vinnie and Jonas – sat down for their last supper, they knew the parting of ways would be an emotional one and that they had all made friends for life. Last woman standing Stephanie Beacham told them she had 'never been teased so much since I was ten. I laughed like a child, I felt like a child. You've been like teasing brothers.'

Footballer-turned-film-star Vinnie chipped in, 'It's been a wonderful experience and it's one we'll look back on.'

'This has been an emotional rollercoaster for me,' Alex told the group. 'I came in here with a lot of misconceptions in the press about me. I was quite naive. But I have listened to things you [Vinnie and Stephanie] and Stephen have told me and I've taken on board things you've said to me.'

Perhaps most surprisingly, Alex had made a great new friend in Katie's ex.

'We've spent four weeks together and had no problem,' Dane told *new!* magazine, after leaving the house. 'The situation has totally changed and to be honest, Alex had to deal with a few things in there that would have been hard, such as talking about me and Katie. He dealt with it like an absolute gent, he was very dignified.

'I can't think of a time when he was vindictive or horrible to anyone in the house.'

Dane admitted he'd thought Alex was a 'bit of a Doris' for the first week they were together, but concluded, 'He's a good lad.'

Stephanie was the first to leave the house on the final day, describing her time inside as 'blissful'. Then came Jonas and Vinnie, leaving Dane and Alex in the house alone. The tense twosome sat side by side on the sofa, awaiting the announcement of the winner's name and making the occasional comment to each other.

After a few excruciating minutes, Davina named Alex as the winner of *Celebrity Big Brother* 2010 and Dane gave his new pal a huge hug, congratulating him on the victory.

'I'm very, very happy that Alex won,' he told Davina after he exited the house. 'The best line I've ever heard about him is he's a lovable prat. He's his own man. He's a gentleman.'

Alex had secured a whopping 65.9 per cent of the votes, to Dane's 34.1 per cent. The victor, who had been booed and abused on his way in, walked out of the house to a barrage of cheers and signs reading 'We love Alex' and 'Well done, Alex'. In just four weeks, he had gone from cross-dressing cage fighter and Katie Price's boyfriend to a national hero. But, as he walked down the stairs, scanning the crowd, only one thought was foremost in his mind – was she there? The public now loved him, but did she?

'It was upsetting to think she might not be there,' he later said to *Star* magazine. 'I was so desperate to see her. I was looking for her in the audience and thinking, "Where is she? Where is she?" Then I saw her, I thought, "Cor, she looks fit in that short skirt." I felt like a kid at Christmas. I just wanted to eat her all up at once.'

The amazingly warm welcome from the *Big Brother* crowd left Alex stunned and emotional. 'I'm very overwhelmed. What an amazing, fantastic start to a new year,' he told Davina in his exit interview. 'I'm not getting booed now. That's amazing … I'm speechless. My whole agenda in here was to be myself.'

Having stated in the Diary Room that he wanted to find 'the real Alex Reid', the new *CBB* winner was asked who that really is. 'He's a man, he's passionate, he's going to win a fight in three months. I'm a fighter and I'm a man in love.'

But he was dismayed when the cheers turned to boos as soon as Katie's name was mentioned, and he quashed any doubts about their relationship with a romantic declaration. 'Come on, guys, don't do that,' he told the baying mob. 'I'm sorry, guys … I'm not sorry – I really love Katie Price!'

On the subject of Dane Bowers, he was just as complimentary as the singer would be about him. 'I was surprised by what a cool dude he is,' Alex commented. 'I'm really looking forward to seeing more of Dane.'

Over in the *Big Brother's Big Mouth* studio, Katie was delighted that her lovers, past and present, had ended in the top two, taking that as a vindication of her taste in men.

'Alex went in there and everyone thought he was this and that,' she said. 'I'd also like to say, I know I've been out with Dane as well. The two guys I've been with have been the last two. It goes to show they're genuine guys. I don't go for shitheads, basically.'

She brushed off the booing, saying, 'It's panto, I love it,' and mirrored Alex's declaration with one of her own. 'We've just spent the past twenty minutes in the other room catching up. He's the love of my life and he knows that. There's a long reason behind [me breaking up with him before] and he knows that. After the jungle, we were back together after four days and he lives with me.'

The four weeks apart while Alex had been in the *CBB* house had been painful for both of them. Katie admitted that she had had just as many doubts as Alex during their period of separation, wondering if he would reject her on his exit, exactly as she had done a few months earlier when she'd dropped out of *I'm a Celebrity … Get Me Out of Here!*

'When he was in the house, we were both worrying that the other one didn't want to be with them,' she told *OK!* magazine. 'How sweet is that?

I took Michelle [Heaton] down to the studios for an appearance and I was pleading with them to let me in the Diary Room so I could be nearer to him. I was asking the producers, "Has he gone off me?" But they told me, "No, he talks about you all the time."'

Alex, in turn, had missed her every day he was away.

'It was so painful,' he said in their joint interview with *OK!* 'It wasn't nice. I missed her all the time. Especially in the morning and at night when there was no one to cuddle.'

Reunited at last, and with the balance of their relationship dramatically altered by Alex's new-found fame and popularity, the couple prepared to go forward with their love and their life together, more solid than ever before.

CHAPTER TWELVE

PRICEY'S MR RIGHT

'I 'VE COMPLETELY REALIZED how fantastic she is, how generous and kind she is, and how much I fancy her. She is the perfect woman for me,' said Alex to *Star*.

After four weeks apart, the *CBB* winner was ready to settle down for good. His conversation with Nicola in the *BB* house, about how to choose suitable rings, had been a bit of a giveaway as to the train of his private thoughts. Even though he complained that Katie was 'stressful' to buy for because she could 'buy the whole shop', it was obvious that a special shopping trip would be on the cards before too long. With the memory of his ill-fated dash to Australia still fresh in his mind, Alex was keen to seal the deal and get a ring on Katie's finger as soon as possible.

Judging by her effusive sentiment about him, this time there was no danger of anything going wrong.

'He's perfect in every way,' she told *OK!* magazine. 'He's a proper gentleman, he's well-built. I feel protected. And he's not show muscles – his muscles are there for a reason. He's protective; he's like my shining knight in armour.'

Asked about marriage plans, Katie went one step further and started planning a whole new family. 'Yes. This year I will marry Alex and I'm going to have his kids,' she replied.

'It's been a fantastic start to the New Year and it's going to be even more fantastic now this is happening,' added her besotted bloke. 'I actually asked Katie to marry me after my fight in September, so it's something we've been discussing for some time.'

And Katie promised that this time she would become Mrs Reid in all aspects of life, vowing to change the name on her passport and chequebook, and share everything. She even pledged to sell her £2.5 million mansion and downsize to a smaller home that they could go halves on.

In the same interview, Alex revealed that housemates Dane and Vinnie had added to his doubts about their relationship during the course of the TV show.

'I was locked away for four weeks with no contact with her and that was the most painful thing,' he recalled. 'You start thinking, "Is she going to be there when I come out?" The guys were questioning me about how strong our relationship is. It's human nature to wonder, but before I went in, Katie said, "Whatever happens, I'll be here waiting for you and I love you."' That was all he'd had to cling on to for the four long weeks in the house.

Vinnie himself admitted that the two men had been less than enthusiastic about the romance, but claimed he was trying to protect 'Rocky' from being hurt. 'We were sitting on the fence because we didn't know whether she was gonna dump him or not,' he told Alan Carr on *Alan Carr: Chatty Man*. 'Dane and I were trying to prepare him. I was really happy for Alex when he won. I just hope he can keep a lid on it all – but he does really love her.'

Despite his former housemates' concerns, Alex was handling his new-found fame – and his high-profile relationship – brilliantly. Katie in particular was impressed by the way he was coping and was convinced that his sudden popularity would not change him one bit. 'He's so grounded,' she said to *OK!* 'Fame doesn't faze him.'

Upon leaving the *CBB* house, Alex had plenty to say about his fellow contestants. In general, he felt he had come away with some really good friends – as well as a touch of religion and a possible Hollywood career. Both Stephen Baldwin and Vinnie Jones had promised him a helping hand in LaLa Land and Alex was chomping at the bit.

'I'm flabbergasted and really happy they are doing that,' he commented to *new!* magazine. 'It's the most amazing thing in the world. I didn't go there to network, I went there to show myself. But I have come out with all these amazing gifts. I still have a cage fight at the end of May, so I am focusing on that at the moment, but in the back of my mind, I am thinking, "I'm an actor. I have done a few bits here and there and this is the perfect opportunity to get back into it."'

It was something that was clearly foremost in his mind as he had also mentioned it in his exit interview with Davina, saying, 'Vinnie has been very inspirational to me. He's transitioned from athletic [*sic*] to actor, which is what I want to do.'

On the subject of religion, Alex said he had been intrigued by his deep and meaningful conversation with born-again Christian Stephen and revealed to *OK!* magazine, 'I definitely want to look into it more.'

Reassuring everyone that he was not about to transform into some kind of 'Bible-basher', he couldn't deny his fascination with the idea of a higher power. And he wasn't afraid to discuss his spiritual side in public, commenting to the mag, 'It's considered taboo and not cool to talk about Jesus and God, but what's the big deal?' Stephen Baldwin had challenged Alex in the house on his views, and the actor had clearly given the cage fighter pause for thought.

The newly supportive Katie even suggested she may soon be spending her Sunday mornings in church, rather than sleeping off her Saturday nights: 'If Alex wanted to do that, he could get me interested, yeah,' she said to *OK!* magazine.

Alex had nothing but praise for Hollywood star Stephanie Beacham, who 'amazed' him with stories of her glittering career, and he thought Jonas was 'such a zany character ... a bit of a stud as well'.

The only housemate he was not so keen on was LA madam Heidi Fleiss. Told that she had said she thought Alex was gay and that Katie should dump him, he bit back via *OK!*, 'She should get rid of herself. She's not exactly normal, is she? I saw her documentary – not a nice person by the look of it.'

He reiterated his astonishment at the fact that he and Dane got on so well and was optimistic about their friendship being a lasting one. 'I was surprised at how cool he is and what a gentleman he is,' he told *new!* magazine. 'He's a friend for life.'

Dane clearly felt the same about the longevity of the friendship, revealing to *new!* in his own interview that the pals had already made plans to stay in touch. Alex was even trying to help Dane embark on a fitness regime. As the duo live close to one another, it was the perfect arrangement – although Dane confessed, 'He's trying to train me up, but I'm too lazy.'

The friendship was good evidence of Alex's laid-back and easygoing nature. Dane and *BB* 'boss' Vinnie had occasionally ganged up on the fighter inside the house, but Alex let that slide, saying they had actually taught him a lot. In his exit interview with Davina, he revealed, 'I have taken on board what Vinnie and Dane have said to me. They have made me think, "Yeah, I can act like a plonker sometimes." I know I am not hurting anyone, but maybe I am hurting myself.'

Indeed, he was full of respect for what the unique experience of *Big Brother* had taught him. The time away from the glaring media spotlight – even as his actions were broadcast to the nation – had given him time to think, to grow and to learn. 'I have actually grown in there. I have matured. It's weird to say that,' he mused to Davina. 'I've not become more intelligent – but I've become more wise.'

While her ex and her current man had been bonding in the house, Katie had been watching at home, finding the whole experience surreal. 'It was strange watching them in the *BB* house because Dane was talking about me when Alex wasn't there,' she said on *GMTV*, adding pleasantly, 'but we all get on like a house on fire.'

The besotted girlfriend also revealed that she had been glued to the live feed from the *Big Brother* house and had got her fix of Alex each night without fail. 'I couldn't go to bed until he went to bed.' And, although she was relieved he didn't 'get it out' on national TV, she found Alex's penchant for stripping off in front of the cameras highly amusing, if not surprising.

'He's quite an exhibitionist, that's why we suit each other because I am too,' she told Alan Carr on his chat show. Echoing Alex's mum's earlier revelations, she laughed about her lover's topless breakfasts at home and concluded, 'I'm not complaining, he's got a fit body.'

She did have one complaint, though, it seems. While her beau was in the *Big Brother* house, she had been waiting for Alex to declare his love for her publicly. Given that she'd banned him from talking about their relationship, however, it may have been an unfair expectation.

'All I wanted him to say was, "Oh, I really love Kate," and every night when I was watching it, I'm like, "Say it, say it," because I'm pining for him. He never did, but we made up for it after,' she said to the Press Association.

With his rounds of post-show interviews over, Alex was finally able to whisk his woman off to the Pennyhill Park Hotel, a luxury venue set in acres of Surrey countryside. Together they enjoyed a gourmet dinner in the hotel's Michelin-starred restaurant and a walk in the beautiful grounds, as well as taking advantage of the luxury spa. Most of all, they simply relished the chance to relax together, away from the prying eyes of the world, and to spend time alone.

The *Big Brother* victory, and its implications, had hardly sunk in yet, but Alex had other things on his mind. The woman he had battled for and almost lost just two months before was back in his arms – and, this time, it was for keeps. It had been a rough ride for the seven months that they had known each other, but Alex was a fighter and had been adamant, after a mere two weeks of their relationship, that Katie Price was The One for him. Now he rated 'winning the love of this lovely lady' as a more important achievement than securing the coveted *Celebrity Big Brother* crown.

But the win meant things had changed – and for the better. The balance of the relationship had shifted. He was no longer the latest fame-hungry hunk on Jordan's arm, but a much-loved celebrity in his own right, with a glittering future in front of him. Whether it was as a fighter, a presenter or even, as Stephen Baldwin had suggested, the next James Bond, any opportunities offered now would be because he is Alex Reid, a celebrity by his own merit.

The biggest relief was escaping the tired old tag 'cross-dressing cage fighter', a phrase that had plagued him for months. 'I want to be seen as more than that,' he said to *OK!* magazine. 'I want to be something substantial in my life. This is an opportunity to get away from that. It makes me and Katie more equal and more strong. When there is that imbalance of careers, maybe resentment can build on both sides. In the future, that could've been a possibility. But not now.'

Katie, for her part, was thrilled that he had won – and, perhaps most importantly, had shown the whole nation the very qualities that had made her fall in love with him in the first place. Part of her hoped that the public might now understand their relationship, or that they would at least appreciate that she and Alex were a real couple in love, and that the affair was not some publicity stunt staged to garner extra column inches.

At the same time, she was slightly apprehensive about where Alex's new fame might take him, however. She insisted to *OK!*, 'Alex isn't the kind of person to let his head swell. He's still grounded.' Pragmatically, though, she reasoned, 'If he changes, he changes.' And, true to form, the PR genius had a savvy tip for her media-virgin man, which contained an urgent message: 'He needs to milk it while he can.'

Pilloried in the press ever since her messy split

from Pete, some small part of Katie was no doubt hoping that some of Alex's new popularity would rub off on her. While she had dismissed the boos and jeers she had received at the *Celebrity Big Brother* final as 'panto', she was privately hurt that the turnaround in her man's credibility hadn't won her any more fans of her own.

'She might say it doesn't, but that abuse would bother anyone,' claimed Alex in his interview with *new!* magazine. 'She probably lies to herself and me about that. We all would.'

Protective Alex felt that some of his joy was marred by the reaction of the crowd towards the woman he loves. 'She's my girlfriend, I love her and I don't want to see her suffer like that. Perhaps I can help change that now, I hope I can,' he mused to *Star* magazine.

And he pleaded with the public to remember their change of heart in his case, and try to apply the same viewpoint to his lover. 'I just hope the public learns something from this. Four weeks ago, I was the bad guy getting booed; now they're cheering me. They got it wrong about me – and they got it wrong about Katie.'

Secluded in their romantic hideaway, the

star-crossed lovers were planning the next step in their relationship. Having caught up with the news, and talked deeply over dinner, they had decided their future together.

The next day, a coy Katie was sporting a huge sparkler on her ring finger and was keen to tell the world they were getting married in 2010. This time, she vowed, she was keeping some things private and it would not be a 'Katie and Peter relationship'. When asked by *OK!* magazine what kind of wedding it would be, Katie stated simply, 'That's for later.'

Within days, the couple had made their next move – and it was one that would take even the most avid Jordan-watchers by surprise.

CHAPTER THIRTEEN

A NEW FAIRY TALE

N SEPTEMBER 2005, Katie Price had married Peter Andre in one of the most lavish weddings in the showbiz world. The £250,000 Cinderella-themed ceremony at Highclere Castle in Berkshire saw the blushing bride arrive in an outrageous pumpkin-style coach and emerge in a huge, pink princess dress to walk down the aisle. Her dress had the longest train on the planet, while the bodice of the gown was encrusted with thousands of Swarovski crystals. Bridesmaids included Michelle Heaton, Kerry Katona and Girls Aloud star Sarah Harding … and the whole bash was spread over two issues of a glossy magazine.

Five years later, Katie walked down the aisle again in a very different ceremony, tucked away in a chapel in Las Vegas and hidden from the eyes of the world.

Before leaving the UK, the unusually reticent

couple would reveal only that they were off on a five-day break overseas, so that Alex could recharge his batteries and spend some one-on-one time with Katie before embarking on his next challenge, a martial arts show due to be filmed in India. Katie's close pals Gary Cockerill and Phil Turner, among the few people aware of their wedding plans, secretly flew out to join them in 'Sin City' to give the glamour girl away; press co-ordinator Diana Colbert was also invited. But the do was so hush-hush that even the couple's families weren't told.

On 2 February 2010, the day of the wedding, the bride and groom shopped for rings at jeweller TeNo beneath the Planet Hollywood Hotel, where they were staying. After some deliberation, they settled on a steel-and-diamond Yunis ring for Alex and a modest platinum band for Katie. Then the couple enjoyed a pre-wedding tipple of champagne and shared some chocolate-dipped strawberries, before returning to their lavish suite in the hotel to prepare for the nuptials.

At 4 p.m., Katie walked down a rose-strewn aisle in the nearby Wynn Hotel, on the arms of Gary and Phil, who were giving her away. Instead of the vast pink meringue of five years before, Katie wore an elegant off-the-peg wedding dress and Alex dressed in a cream suit and shirt. Katie smiled at her groom and held his hand under a canopy of trees, between two beautiful fountains. In a 22-minute ceremony, the couple were declared man and wife and sealed the deal with a passionate kiss.

After posing for private photographs, the elated newlyweds phoned their families to break the news to them. While Katie's mum Amy had her doubts about the wisdom of the move, she ultimately supported her daughter's decision and realized how much in love the couple were.

Bob and Carol Reid were surprised and delighted. 'We had no idea, but we're so happy for him. This is what he has always wanted,' Carol told the *Daily Star*. 'He called in the middle of the night and I spoke to both of them. They were really, really happy. There is no disappointment for us about not being there, we are just genuinely pleased for them.'

'This is magical for him,' added her husband.

With Diana's help, the couple also issued a joint statement to the press announcing their marriage and declaring, 'Katie and Alex are delighted to announce they got married in a private, simple ceremony.

'We are very much in love. We look forward to the future together. We can't wait to get back and celebrate our marriage with our friends and family, who fully support our wishes.'

In the face of cynical questions about the union, Katie's agent was forced to deny rumours of a magazine deal. 'Their decision to marry has not been made with any media deal in place,' she said. 'It is purely down to their love for each other.'

Having informed their nearest and dearest, along with the world's press, of the happy news, the bride and groom got on with their wedding reception ... in a nearby strip club. Mr and Mrs Reid reportedly spent three hours in the Sapphire Club, before heading back to their suite – which came with its own dance pole – for a wedding supper of oysters, creamy rock shrimp and crispy rice with tuna, from the hotel's Japanese restaurant, Koi. They followed their meal with a sumptuous, molten chocolate cake with fresh berries and a bottle of Dom Perignon champagne.

Alex, who had now landed his own column in *Star* magazine, was clearly over the moon to have wed the woman of his dreams. 'So, me and Katie have done it – we're married!' he wrote. 'I feel incredibly happy. After winning *Celebrity Big Brother* and then this, I've had the best week of my life. I don't want to go into too much detail, but Katie, of course, looked stunning.'

He confirmed that the couple had celebrated their marriage in the Sapphire Gentlemen's Club, revealing that it is owned by a friend of his and that his pal had kindly invited them to celebrate there. 'It was a real laugh – a bit tongue-in-cheek – and, of course, we had loads of champagne there. But it wasn't just topless girls – the gay mafia were out in force, too – and it was actually a nice sort of family atmosphere. It was a big night, as you can imagine!'

The new lifestyle that Alex now found himself living was clearly agreeing with him. His description of their penthouse suite in the Planet Hollywood Hotel, which came complete with a butler to attend to their every need, made him sound like a kid in a sweet shop. 'We stayed in the penthouse suite at the Planet Hollywood Hotel, which is like three apartments in one. Our room had the best view across the Strip and our bed was enormous – like a football pitch! And we had a butler on call at all times. I'm so lucky and feel very blessed at the moment.'

Back home, Katie's ex and Alex's new BFF Dane

Bowers was full of congratulations, although his comments were not all complimentary. 'I hope it works, not least because there are kids involved,' he told *Reveal*. 'I think they're well suited. I'll always care for Katie because I know how nice she can be. But so often she ruins it and I don't think anyone around her is honest at all.'

Warming to his theme, he continued, 'Surely you'd tell her, "You're an absolute k**b," for some of the things she comes out with. I would and she knows that. I wouldn't like to see anything really horrible said about her, but sometimes I just think she's asking for it.'

Across the Atlantic, all Katie was asking for was some quality time with her new husband. The day after the wedding, a late brunch was sent to the newlyweds' room before Alex popped to the gym and Katie finally emerged for a £235 steak dinner. A day of buggy racing in the Nevada desert kept things on the fast track for another day – but the honeymoon was sadly to be short-lived.

Just three days after saying 'I do', Alex had to jet off to Mumbai to face tough martial arts training and a bout against eight expert fighters for his Bravo show *Alex Reid: The Fight of His Life*. His bride, meanwhile, was due to fly home to start a fresh round of interviews to promote the latest series of her ITV reality show, *What Katie Did Next*.

The blissful happiness that the new Mrs Reid was enjoying in Las Vegas was also set to be all too brief. In her absence from the UK, the tabloid headlines had soon switched from her Vegas 'quickie' wedding to focus, once again, on her ex-husband Peter Andre. The day after Katie's shock nuptials, the Australian singer had admitted that he and the kids had known nothing of her plans and, when quizzed on Sky News about his children's relationship with their new stepfather, he had broken down in tears.

'I was doing a signing in Basildon and someone told me [about the wedding]. But it's not my business,' he told interviewer Kay Burley. 'To be honest, I wasn't surprised at all. Just like any other parent, what I care about is whether they are a good influence on my children.'

Clearly comparing Peter's new situation with that of Harvey and Dwight Yorke when Peter married Katie, Kay went on to ask what he would say if Alex asked to adopt Junior and Princess Tiaamii, as Pete had adopted Harvey.

'No one is going to take my kids away from me

– nobody. I'm sorry,' answered Peter forcefully, with tears in his eyes. 'Nobody is going to take my kids away from me. And I will fight to the death for that. Nobody's going to take those kids away – I'll die before I let that happen. It's not going to happen. I will go to court.'

A clip was then shown of Dwight calling Peter's request to adopt Harvey 'disrespectful', sending the doting dad over the edge.

'No disrespect, but has he seen Harvey since that interview?' fumed Pete. 'I love that child, I see that child, and to me a nice little "thank you" would be nice. I asked to adopt him because I loved him, I didn't ask to adopt him to be disrespectful. When you love a child … He's in my life, he calls me "Dad". I never said I'm his father, but I'm so proud to have him in my life.'

Pete, who had been appearing on the programme to promote his new album, then asked for the interview to be stopped and fled backstage, where Kay later revealed that he had 'sobbed'. But she concluded on her blog that the two of them, despite the upsetting line of questioning, had parted amicably. She also commented that he had come across as a 'devoted dad'.

Yet some observers wondered if it was Pete's devotion to the kids that had sent him over the edge … or a broken heart. Had Pete – who had himself remained so transparently single ever since the day he split from Katie – been moved to tears by the news that his ex-wife had already remarried, not even a year after their divorce? It would be difficult news for many people.

But in a separate interview, Peter was adamant that his tears had absolutely nothing to do with the wedding – and even claimed to be pleased that his ex had tied the knot again. 'I wasn't upset because of the wedding, absolutely not,' he insisted in the *News of the World*. 'To me, it was the best closure I could have asked for. Once she became Mrs Reid, it's not my business any more. I stepped away from the circus a long time ago. Whatever is to do with the kids will be my business.'

While Katie may have been frustrated that Pete had somehow managed to make himself into the good guy in all this – yet again – she had clearly decided to change tack when it came to her ex. In a *GMTV* interview on 9 February, she amazed everybody by coming out in support of Pete and defending him to the hilt.

'I heard about the Sky News thing,' she said. 'I thought it was so cruel, so out of order. They can't compare Pete and Dwight at all. Pete has been there, he's been like [Harvey's] dad, and he's fantastic with him.'

Alex, meanwhile, used his new column to reassure the kids' father that he had nothing to worry about. 'I really feel for him,' he wrote. 'I've got no animosity towards him and I'm not after the kids at all. I'd like to sit down with him and for us all to be friends.'

At the same time as supporting her ex, Katie was keen to praise her new husband's relationship with her children, saying on the TV show, 'Alex is great. I would never go out with any man unless he accepted my children. He's like a manny [male nanny]. He's fantastic with them, especially with Harvey, because Harvey is a challenge.'

The *GMTV* interview naturally touched on the recent big news in Katie's personal life, which had been the number-one topic of water-cooler gossip ever since the news had hit the week before. Looking a little more subdued than usual, and clearly on the back foot, Katie felt forced to defend her new marriage just seven days after walking down the aisle. When her plane had landed at Heathrow, Katie had come back down to earth with a cruel bump. She was horrified to find that the reports on her wedding ranged from sneering to downright nasty, and talk of a magazine deal had really cheapened the couple's private romantic day.

On the show, she rubbished reports that had appeared in a downmarket newspaper that the whole thing was a publicity stunt and purely for money, railing in frustration, 'There is no magazine deal. We've just got married, we're so happy, and they're trying to put a downer on it. They treat me like a serial killer. What have I actually done wrong? That's my point.'

She also explained the decision to elope to Vegas, which was in fact the only place where it was legal for the couple to wed so soon after Katie's divorce. The duo had originally planned for their nuptials to take place in the Caribbean, but the legal requirements vetoed this intention. Conscious of the stereotype of what a Vegas wedding is like, and wanting to defend the happiest day of her life, Katie went out of her way to insist that there had been nothing trashy about the ceremony whatsoever, saying to Kate Garraway that, 'There were no Elvises or anything and it wasn't tacky – in fact, the pictures were gorgeous.

'It was just for us. It wasn't controlled, it was just what me and Alex wanted to do and we had a brilliant day. It was like a dream.'

Like many brides, Katie wanted the celebrations of their union to go on and on. And, with the wedding having been such an intimate, private event, she had the perfect excuse to keep partying. She revealed that the newlyweds planned to organize a bigger, flashier bash to celebrate the marriage sometime in the summer, for the benefit of the pair's families.

'We are going to do a big blessing thing because of our families. We want Princess to be a bridesmaid, and for his mum and family [to be involved], but as it stands, we haven't done a magazine deal at all.'

And that may be the way it stays. Throughout all her interviews to plug her new reality show, which covered her journey from the jungle to the Las Vegas chapel, Katie maintained that the new marriage would be a much more private affair than her previous romance. And she hinted that having cameras following her and Pete around day after day for their own fly-on-the-wall series had marred their life together.

'[Alex and I have] done the odd shoot, but it's not going to be like it was with me and Pete, no way,' she told Radio 1's Chris Moyles. '[Alex has] got his own career and I have my own career: it's separate. And no one is controlling us, saying when we can hold hands, when we can't hold hands, say this in an interview, say that. It was controlled. When I watch *Pop Idol* or *X Factor*, I know it's all manufactured, and with Pete, it was true love, but we were manufactured as well. That's why I got out of it, that's why I left. It was too much.'

The Las Vegas wedding, she pledged, would remain a private exchanging of vows between two people in love. Other than the low-key photographs belonging to the newlyweds, there was no other pictorial record of the day. Katie insisted that there had been no TV cameras at the ceremony, either – in a more down-to-earth manner, the duo had simply got an ordinary wedding video to commemorate the event, which had been supplied by the chapel. Taking no chances, Katie said both video and snaps were kept securely at her home, locked up in her private safe.

And she refused to release any details about Alex's September proposal, saying only, 'He proposed to me, but I'm not saying how it happened. It's not a Pete and Kate relationship – things are private and mysterious between us. I have learnt from my mistakes.'

Now that she was 'legally Mrs Reid', she was keen to call a truce with her ex-husband and hoped that one day he could be friends with Alex. She insisted she held no grudges against Pete and wished they would all start talking again. Asked what she would say to him if she had the chance, she said candidly: 'We're not in the kids' playground, we're fully grown adults, there's kids involved, let's be adult about it.'

The kids were central to both Katie and Pete. And after Peter's outburst on Sky News about the children, she was at pains to reassure her ex that he had absolutely nothing to worry about as far as the kids were concerned, calling him 'an amazing dad' and confirming that Alex had no plans to adopt the children. She finished with an optimistic vision of the future: '[Alex and I are] going to have our own kids. And hopefully one day Pete will come round and he'll have kids with his girlfriend and we can all play happy families.' Well, who knows? It might just happen.

For his part, Pete – who had finally had the tattoo bearing the name of his ex removed from his finger – stated that he had no problem with Alex, but no desire to talk to him either. 'I have no problem with him. I've never met the guy. I just don't see a reason why I have to sit down and have a chat at this point,' he told the *News of the World*.

On her return home, Katie was aware that it was now time to break the news to the children that she had moved on from their dad. Although the actual split between her and Pete had taken place some eight months before, the children were too young to grasp the full situation and had been continuing to believe that they were spending time with one parent while the other was working.

'It's like Santa Claus,' Pete had explained on Sky News. 'You kind of let them believe everything's OK until the point they have to know. Maybe that time has come.'

Indeed it had, and Katie did her best, revealing later to the Press Association that she had told son Junior about the wedding. 'But what do you say to a four-year-old, what do they understand?' she said. Referring to Princess Tiaamii, she added, 'And certainly a two-year-old wouldn't understand; and Harvey is more interested in his cake.'

Like any newlywed, Katie was, in general, over the moon and dreaming of the future, making big plans for her, her new husband and their family. Nevertheless, two things clouded her happy horizon. As ever, she was wounded by the reaction in the press and furious that many papers were attacking their marriage just a week after Alex had slipped the ring on her finger. But that was the media, and Katie had long experience of hardening her heart against the worst excesses and even the most hurtful commentaries from the press.

More painful to her by far, however, was the fact that Alex was so many miles away. Used to being forced apart by their respective careers, she took his absence in her stride – but facing the media hostility and the probing personal questions without her husband was not exactly how she had wanted to start their marriage, to say nothing of the fact that she longed to be with him and missed him dreadfully, with every beat of her lonely heart.

Meanwhile, on a different continent, Alex – who was somewhat secluded from the media scrum, although paparazzi shots of him abroad trickled back to the UK on a regular basis – was training hard in a remote area of India, where he had been suffering from a vicious stomach bug. Despite the health setback, a tough fight – against eight opponents in one go – was due to go ahead. There was no time to reflect on his new marital status, no moment to relish his happiness. He had to knuckle down and focus: reality was back with a bite.

In short, for both newlyweds, it was proving a tough time. They could only talk on the phone and wish they were together. But Katie, for one, was determined that careers would not get in the way of her marriage this time.

Asked by the Press Association how she would respond if forced to choose between her husband and her fame, Katie replied instantly, 'Alex! I'm Mrs Reid now, Mrs Reid all the way. I'm doing marriage properly this time. To me, it's more important now to have my family life, my husband.

'I'm doing it completely differently this time.'

CHAPTER FOURTEEN

TOGETHER FOREVER

WHATEVER THE PAPERS were saying about the newlyweds, Katie herself was convinced that Alex was the love of her life and that, this time, they would be 'together forever'. To prove the point, she took one vital decision – which clearly demonstrated her trust and love for Alex – and refused to consider a pre-nuptial agreement. With Pete, the documents had been drawn up and signed in advance of the wedding, but Katie had always privately considered these legal agreements to be unromantic. Despite her vast fortune, estimated at £30 million, and Alex's relatively small pot in contrast, she wouldn't hear of a pre-nup. She was playing for keeps.

Very shortly after Katie and Alex tied the knot, the blushing bride had realized that she couldn't face another two weeks away from her new husband so soon after the *Celebrity Big Brother* separation, not to mention the fact that the duo wanted to remain together on their post-nuptial cloud nine for as long as possible. But it wasn't to be. Immediately after the wedding, Katie attempted to get a visa to join Alex in India. But, sadly, they had left the crucial paperwork too late. Consequently, as Katie faced the music at home, alone, Alex was on an emotional rollercoaster some 4,500 miles away.

'Although my trip away has been amazing,' he wrote in his *Star* column, 'I have missed my new wife terribly, and I know she has missed me a lot too. It's been hard to be apart, but absence makes the heart grow fonder.'

He admitted that the separation was not as tough as it had been while he was on *Celebrity Big Brother* because, this time, he was able to talk to his missus on the phone, and had been doing so a lot. On the other side of the world, Alex was unwell, with 'agonizing stomach cramps' so painful he thought he was having a hernia; he was off his food and in a foreign country. But despite the strange and uncomfortable circumstances, his euphoria at his new marital state hadn't worn off in the slightest.

'I am still feeling so happy,' he continued. 'It

has finally all sunk in now and being married to Mrs Reid is the most amazing thing in the world.' His only complaint was that he had to remove his wedding ring to fight.

At home in Surrey, surrounded by her kids once more, Katie was busy during the day with little time to stop and think. At night, with the kids asleep in bed, she longed for Alex's comforting cuddles and couldn't wait to talk to him on the phone.

Tucking in her children each evening, there was another thought utmost in her mind, as well as in her absent husband's. Both were already craving additions to the family. Alex, who adores his three stepchildren, has always wanted kids of his own.

'Being one of six, he's always loved children,' his mum said to the *Sunday Mirror*, while her son was in the *Celebrity Big Brother* house. 'And Alex is quite happy with Katie's. But he's thirty-four now and broody. His body clock is ticking.'

Happily, Alex's new wife seemed just as eager to start procreating. Katie was excitedly telling everyone she spoke to that she was chomping at the bit to start producing more babies. Alex was reportedly keen to have three children, and she was more than happy to go along with his plans, claiming she'd always wanted a big family. Katie had even coined a new word for the forthcoming impregnation!

'I can't wait to be Reidinated,' she chuckled to the Press Association. 'We're absolutely dying to have a baby. I'm so hoping that by the end of this series [of *What Katie Did Next*] that I can announce that I'm pregnant ... I so can't wait to get preggie. So watch out for the bump.'

Alex was excited by the prospect of a growing family as well and was keen to hear the patter of tiny feet – male or female. He was quite enjoying trying for a baby, too. 'I can confirm that we did a lot of practising in Vegas!' he joked in his column.

In the meantime, with the couple separated by thousands of miles, not a lot of practising was going on at all and, as Valentine's Day approached, Alex had to break it to his missus that she would be spending the romantic occasion alone. Katie had already told Pete he could have the kids, so he was looking forward to spending the day with 'my beautiful little Princess'.

'I'm over the moon that I will be spending Valentine's Day with the kids,' an excited Pete, who was planning to bake cupcakes with all three children, said to *OK!* magazine. 'Princess is my little pretty flower.'

In an emotional phone call from India, Alex apologized to his wife for not being there for their first Valentine's Day and promised to make it up to her as soon as he got back. Unfortunately, filming on the Bravo show would not be over in time for him to fly home – and instead he would be sharing a hotel room with his manager. It was hardly the romantic scenario the newlyweds might have envisaged for their first 14 February together.

On the date itself, however, Alex pulled a blinder. Unable to make an appearance himself, he nevertheless managed to brighten up Katie's lonely day with an unexpected and flamboyant gift. As Katie mooched around at home, desperately missing her man, no less than three boxes – containing personal mementos, framed pictures of the two of them, flowers and chocolates – arrived on their doorstep. If he couldn't be with her, at least he wasn't going to let her think he didn't care.

'WOW three huge boxes turned up ....my husband really has spoilt me for valentines day he is just PERFECT..i love you husband amazing,' she posted on Twitter. Later, she tweeted, 'HAPPY

VALENTINES DAY TO EVERYONE....have a great day xxxx'

Back in India, Alex was at last preparing to fly home to his 'incredible' bride. Despite the agonizingly long time away from his new wife, filming hadn't gone as well as could be expected, as he had been forced to pull out of a fight because he wasn't ready, and, of course, the stomach problems had taken their toll on his energy levels.

But that was a worry for another day. For now, all he cared about was Katie. The day after Valentine's Day, an excited Mrs Katie Reid dressed up to the nines to rush to Heathrow and meet her husband off the plane. Afterwards, she whisked him back to Surrey for an emotional reunion – behind closed doors – and served him a lavish home-cooked meal, something he had been craving since his 'Delhi Belly' had put him off curries 'for a lifetime'.

Tired from travelling and filming, Alex welcomed the opportunity to kick back and relax before starting on another round of interviews. He was back in the arms of his one true love and totally elated. He was also looking forward to being reunited with Katie's kids, and cementing his position as stepdad. In an appearance on Alan Carr's *Chatty Man*, filmed shortly after his return, he opened up about his new fatherly role – but reiterated his intention not to replace Pete in any way.

'I am now officially a stepdad, it's surreal,' he smiled. 'I love those little kids, but I don't want to be their dad like Peter Andre. [However] I would love to be and I am, as we speak, an authoritative figure who can look after them and who cares for them.'

But he realized that his new family situation in itself was nowhere near as surreal as the last twelve months in general, during which time he had gone from an observer of the Jordan spectacle, reading about every aspect of Katie's life in the tabloids, to landing the lead role in the 'panto'.

'I used to see Katie Price in the papers all the time and I couldn't understand it,' he admitted to Alan Carr. 'Why is she in the magazines every bloody week? And I thought the wedding was "Ugh, why's she doing all that?" And now I'm married to her!'

The turnabout in his affairs was extraordinary. Less than a year ago, no one except *Hollyoaks* aficionados or cage-fighting enthusiasts knew who Alex Reid was. Now, he was one of the most famous men in Britain, and was married to one of the nation's most talked about stars. Life wasn't going to quieten down any time soon.

With both Alex and Katie back on home soil in Britain – at long last – the couple certainly looked like they were on cloud nine as they were snapped together, for the first time, in London. Katie, stylishly dressed in a faux fur Russian hat and coat, joined a T-shirt-clad Alex on a freezing cold evening in the capital. A romantic dinner at Nobu and a night in a plush hotel on Park Lane soon made up for the Valentine's Day separation, and onlookers who watched the newlyweds giggle and cuddle their way through dinner could hardly doubt the sincerity of their affection for each other.

The road to true love has been a bumpy one for Katie. Her heartaches and break-ups, well documented along the way, have taken their toll. Her initial fears about her relationship with Alex, which had prompted the shocking rejection on *I'm a Celebrity*, were born of past hurts and painful splits, rather than Alex's faults. The bruising she took over her divorce from Peter would take a while to heal, but Mr Reid certainly seems to be Katie's Mr Right.

His mild-mannered patience is a calming influence on her volatile personality, and his strength a virtue she truly appreciates. 'Normally no one can tell me what to do, but Alex has a way of convincing me,' she told *OK!* 'He's very calming.'

Alex revealed the simple secret to his success to the same magazine: 'I ask her to think about the consequences. It's just basically slowing her down, letting her breathe a bit.'

Alex certainly seemed to have a handle on Katie: her strengths, her weaknesses and her key qualities. He was keenly aware that her impetuous nature and forthright speech – while commendable characteristics in the right context – could occasionally do her more harm than good. 'Sometimes she speaks her mind and sometimes she can be her own worst enemy. Some people don't like the fact she is so outspoken. I think it's great because you always know where you stand. She's very kind and very fair. If you're an arse, Katie will tell you you're an arse.' And if you're the love of her life, she makes that very clear, too.

The couple's temporary split in Australia had served its purpose – in that it had shown Katie, with painful clarity, just how much she loved and needed Alex. Because of that, she insisted, she didn't regret anything she had done in the last year.

'I don't have any regrets about anything. No, not at all,' she said to Digital Spy. 'It's made me the person I am today and put me in the situation I'm in today. I do lots of things right and do lots of things wrong. I'm certainly not perfect and I learn by my mistakes.'

Alex's new TV career had helped to bring balance to the relationship and had also won Katie's trust, as she now believed he was in love with her, not her money or her notoriety.

It was a truth that her new husband, for one, never tired of making clear. 'I need Katie,' he declared passionately to her family and friends via *OK!* magazine, hoping to reassure them once and for all about the integrity of his emotions. 'I don't need her for fame, but I need her.'

For Alex, the more naive and less emotionally battered of the two, the falling had been fast and deep. 'After two weeks, I thought, "This is going to be The One,"' he admitted in their *OK!* interview. 'We've been together for seven months and been through more than most couples go through in a lifetime.'

With their wedding rings now firmly on their fingers, however, the happy couple have braved the worst of the storm and have come through it together, stronger than ever.

Maybe this time the fairy tale will have a happy ending.

ACKNOWLEDGEMENTS

THANKS TO THE following agencies who supplied the images for the plate section.

Page 1: Mirrorpix

Page 2: Rex Features

Page 3: © Gareth Gay/Alpha (top); Getty Images (centre); WENN.com (bottom)

Page 4: Rotello/Rex Features (top); Mirrorpix (bottom)

Page 5: Rex Features (both)

Page 6: Matt Keeble/Splash News (top); Rex Features (bottom)

Page 7: James Cook/Rex Features (top); Rex Features (bottom)

Page 8: Ian Nicholson/PA Wire/Press Association Images

Page 9: WENN.com (top); © Stephen Daniels/Alpha (bottom)

Page 10: Getty Images (top); WireImage/Getty Images (bottom left); WENN.com (bottom right)

Page 11: WireImage/Getty Images

Page 12: Oceanic/Matrixphotos.com (top left); Brian Cassey/Rex Features (centre right); Dennis Stone/ Rex Features (bottom left)

Page 13: Yui Mok/PA Wire/Press Association Images (both)

Page 14: LTVM/FAMOUS

Page 15: Nick Banks/Bigpicturesphoto.com (top); Bigpicturesphoto.com (bottom left); Splash News (bottom right)

Page 16: FilmMagic/Getty Images

SOURCES

THE AUTHOR CONDUCTED her research for this book using a vast range of sources. These listed here were of particular help.

Magazines

Closer

Hello!

Loaded

new!

Now

OK!

Reveal

Star

Newspapers

Daily Star

Mirror

News of the World

The People

The Sun

Sunday Mirror

Radio

The Chris Moyles Show (Radio 1)

TV

Alan Carr: Chatty Man (Openmike Productions)

Big Brother's Big Mouth (Endemol UK)

Celebrity Big Brother 7 (Endemol UK)

Four Weddings (Living TV)

GMTV (GMTV)

The Graham Norton Show (SO Television)

I'm a Celebrity … Get Me Out of Here! (ITV Studios)

I'm a Celebrity … Get Me Out of Here! NOW! (ITV Studios)

Peter Andre: Going It Alone (Can Associates TV)

Sky News (BSkyB)

This Morning (ITV Studios)

What Katie Did Next (ITV Studios/Pricey Media)

Websites

Digital Spy

twitter.com/misskatieprice

With additional acknowledgement to the Press Association.